THE SKYSCRAPER BOOK

To Nathan,
someday you'll have a skyscraper of your own. This should do until then.
♡ Robb

May your love for architecture flourish.

THE SKYSCRAPER BOOK
BY JAMES CROSS GIBLIN

ILLUSTRATIONS BY ANTHONY KRAMER
PHOTOGRAPHS BY DAVID ANDERSON

HarperCollinsPublishers

ACKNOWLEDGMENTS:

For their help with the research for this book, I want to thank the following: the ArchiCenter of Chicago; Daryl W. Boggs; the Commission on Chicago Historical and Architectural Landmarks; Johnson/Burgee Architects, New York; the Landmarks Association of St. Louis; Albert C. Martin and Associates, Los Angeles; the National Trust for Historic Preservation; the New York Public Library; the New York Telephone Company; Jeanne Prahl; radio station WCLV, Cleveland; the Western Reserve Historical Society, Cleveland; the F. W. Woolworth Company; the World Trade Center.

Special thanks to: Marianne Carus, who first encouraged me to write about skyscrapers; Edward Haynes, who taught me how to look at buildings; and my editor, Elizabeth Isele.

Text copyright © 1981 by James Cross Giblin
Illustrations copyright © 1981 by Anthony Kramer
Photographs copyright © 1981 by David Anderson

All rights reserved.
Printed in the United States of America.
No part of this book may be used
or reproduced in any manner whatsoever
without written permission except in
the case of brief quotations embodied
in critical articles and reviews.
For information address HarperCollins
Children's Books, a division of HarperCollins
Publishers, 10 East 53rd Street, New York,
NY 10022.

Library of Congress Cataloging-in-Publication Data

Giblin, James Cross.
   The skyscraper book.

   Summary: Discusses skyscrapers, from the first one constructed in Chicago in 1884 to those of today, and points out the problems skyscrapers have helped solve and create.

   1. Skyscrapers—United States—Juvenile literature.
[1. Skyscrapers] I. Kramer, Anthony. II. Anderson, David. III. Title.
NA6230.G5   1981   725'.23'0973   81-43038
ISBN 0-690-04154-3   AACR2
ISBN 0-690-04155-1 (lib. bdg.)

2 3 4 5 6 7 8 9 10

For my parents, who introduced me to the wonders of cities—including skyscrapers

"The skyscraper is the miracle and monument of the Twentieth Century."

—*Ada Louise Huxtable*

CONTENTS

1: THE VIEW FROM THE TOP *1*

2: THE CHICAGO PIONEERS *6*

3: THE SKYSCRAPER COMES
   TO NEW YORK *16*

4: THE SKYSCRAPER SPREADS
   ACROSS AMERICA *28*

5: THE CHRYSLER BUILDING AND
   THE EMPIRE STATE BUILDING *38*

6: A SKYSCRAPER CITY *48*

7: GLASS BOXES AROUND THE WORLD *54*

8: HIGHER AND HIGHER *64*

9: SKYSCRAPERS IN THE FUTURE *73*

   FABULOUS FACTS ABOUT
   FAMOUS SKYSCRAPERS *76*

   WHAT SOME ARCHITECTURAL TERMS
   MEAN *79*

   BIBLIOGRAPHY *81*

   INDEX *83*

World Trade Center (David Anderson)

1: THE VIEW FROM THE TOP

Every day thousands of tourists from all over the world line up in the blue-carpeted lobby of the World Trade Center in downtown New York City. They are waiting for express elevators that will lift them nonstop to the enclosed observation deck on the 107th floor of the skyscraper.

The deck is 1,310 feet (399 m) above sea level, almost a quarter of a mile up in the sky. From it, huge structures like the Brooklyn Bridge appear to be very small, and cars in the streets below look like tiny toys. Brooklyn lies to the east, New Jersey is to the west, and the Statue of Liberty stands on her island directly to the south. To the northeast can be seen the towers of four other great skyscrapers—the Woolworth Building, the Metropolitan Life Tower, the Empire State Building, and the Chrysler Building. Each, like the World Trade Center, was once the tallest building in the world. Seeing them all together, stretching away in the distance, helps one to understand why the 20th century has often been called "the century of skyscrapers."

The word "skyscraper" didn't always mean a tall building. In the 19th century, it was used for several other things that seemed to "scrape the sky." A skyscraper was the tallest sail on a clipper ship, and high bonnets and hats were also called skyscrapers. So was a baseball that was hit or thrown high into the air. The word was first applied to tall buildings in 1883, when the magazine *American Architect* published a letter saying, "America needs tall buildings; it needs skyscrapers."

Today a building of less than 50 stories or so doesn't seem especially tall. But the first buildings to be called skyscrapers, back in the 1880s, were often only nine or ten stories high. Architects had only just begun to develop the technology needed to construct buildings of more than five or six stories.

For centuries, tall buildings were made of stone. The higher the building, the thicker the walls of the lower floors had to be to support the weight of the upper ones. Then, in the early years of the 19th century, engineers developed sturdy iron frames for bridges, and architects began to use such frames to support the floors of new buildings. But the masonry walls still bore their own weight, and this limited how high a building could go. It wasn't until the 1880s that architects thought of using steel frames sturdy enough to support both the floors *and* the walls of their buildings.

A young Minneapolis architect named L. S. Buffington first dreamed of structures with steel skeletons in 1880. He imagined buildings of 20, 30, 50, and even 100 stories, and drew elaborate sketches of them. Buffington called his buildings "cloud scrapers," and in 1887 he patented engineering calculations for their steel frame construction.

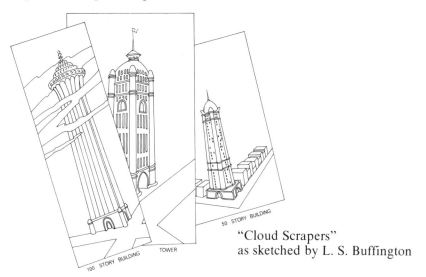

"Cloud Scrapers" as sketched by L. S. Buffington

While Buffington was still dreaming about his cloud scrapers, Major William Le Baron Jenney, a Chicago architect and engineer who had served in the Civil War, was actually using an iron and steel frame in the construction of a tall building. This was the ten-

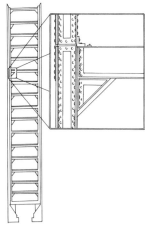

Detail of angle iron bracket construction

story Home Insurance Company Building, which Jenney designed and built in Chicago in 1884. The building had columns of cast iron and crossbeams of iron and steel that were bolted to the columns with angle iron brackets.

According to one story, Major Jenney first realized how strong a steel frame could be when he got angry at the squawkings of the family parrot. He slammed a heavy book down on the parrot's steel wire cage, and was surprised when the wires neither bent nor cracked. Whether that story is true or not, Jenney was the first architect to use a fireproofed frame of iron and steel to support an entire building. Thus he became the builder of the first skyscraper, the simplest definition of which is "a modern building of great height constructed on a steel skeleton."

Steel framing not only meant buildings could rise higher than ever—it had three other advantages over masonry construction. The walls in a building with a steel skeleton could be thinner, leaving more room for rentable shop and office space on all floors. The rooms could be lighter and airier, because there could be more windows in the thinner walls. A building with a steel frame could also be erected more quickly than one built of stone, thereby reducing construction and labor costs.

Steel framing alone would not have made skyscrapers possible, however. Other technological advances were essential to their construction. Especially important was the development of safe passenger elevators, since people could not comfortably climb more than five or six floors.

The inventor Elisha Otis created a sensation when he demonstrated a steam-powered elevator at the Crystal Palace Exhibition in New York in 1853. Accompanied by an assistant, Otis mounted a platform in the central exhibition hall. As a large crowd watched, a cable hoisted the platform high into the air. Then the assistant handed Otis a dagger on a velvet cushion. The crowd gasped and drew back as Otis began to cut through the cable with the dagger. The last fibers separated—but nothing happened; invisible safety catches were holding up the platform. The crowd applauded as Otis descended safely to the floor.

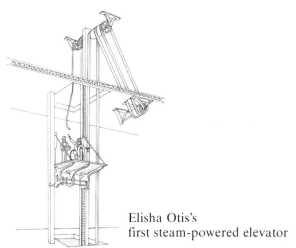

Elisha Otis's first steam-powered elevator

After the exhibition, Otis patented his invention and established a factory to manufacture passenger elevators. In the 1870s, hydraulic elevators operated by water or oil pressure replaced the less efficient steam-powered models. By the late 1880s, lighter and faster electric elevators began to come into use, just when they were needed for the new skyscrapers that were being planned.

The idea of the skyscraper spread quickly in the 1880s because there was a strong need for tall office buildings. After the Civil War in the 1860s, the United States grew rapidly. Immigrants from Europe and people from rural areas streamed into urban areas to fill the jobs that were opening up in factories and offices. As the demand for land in city centers rose, so did real estate prices. Naturally, landlords wanted to have as many floors and as much rentable space as possible in their new buildings. By the 1890s, skyscrapers of nine, ten, 12, and even 14 stories were rising in cities all across America.

Many of these first skyscrapers, including the Home Insurance Company Building, have been demolished over the years to make way for even taller structures. But others are still standing in our cities today. What can we gain from looking at them, and at skyscrapers that were built later? Why, in fact, are skyscrapers important?

Buildings can tell us a lot about people—their dreams, hopes, and needs. Skyscrapers reflect the ambitions of the people who financed their construction and the imagination of the architects who designed them.

Skyscrapers show, too, how people solved the difficult technical problems involved in constructing them. How did engineers dig foundations deep enough and strong enough to anchor the buildings in the ground? How did they support the buildings floor by floor so they could build higher and higher? How did they brace the structures so that they would withstand high winds?

This book tells the stories of the tallest, most famous, and most influential skyscrapers, from the earliest, the Home Insurance Company Building, to the new office towers rising in our cities today. It points out the beauty of skyscrapers—and sometimes their ugliness. It explores the urban problems skyscrapers have helped to solve, and others they've helped to create.

The story does not begin in New York City, which many people mistakenly think of as the birthplace of skyscrapers because there are so many crowded onto Manhattan Island. Instead it begins in the booming city of Chicago in the mid-1800s, just 100 years ago.

2 : THE CHICAGO PIONEERS

A great fire swept through downtown Chicago in 1871, reducing most of the buildings in its path to burned-out shells. After the rubble had been cleared away, business leaders wanted to replace the low brick and wooden structures that had been destroyed with tall new fire-resistant buildings. Tall buildings were badly needed, for the population of Chicago had grown from only 4,000 in 1837 to almost 500,000 in the 1870s as the city had become a great center of railroading and industry.

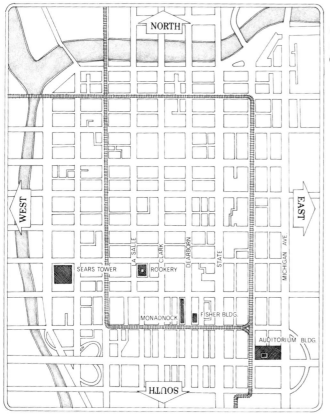

Left: map of "the Loop" in downtown Chicago; *right:* the Rookery (Richard Nickel, courtesy of the Commission on Chicago Historical and Architectural Landmarks)

After the Home Insurance Company Building was erected, one skyscraper after another rose in downtown Chicago in the 1880s and 1890s. They were concentrated near the shore of Lake Michigan in the district that is called "the Loop" because the elevated trains that bring office workers and shoppers in from the suburbs make a loop around it. Today a visitor to Chicago can take a walking tour of the Loop and see a rich sampling of those early skyscrapers.

At the corner of LaSalle and Adams streets stands the Rookery,

erected between 1885 and 1888, and designed by the architectural team of John Wellborn Root and Daniel H. Burnham. The 11-story Rookery got its name from the hundreds of pigeons that had roosted on the temporary city hall and public library that had stood on the site before. Architect Root was amused by the name and made it official by including pigeons and other birds in his designs for the decorative panels to be placed above the entrance of the new building.

The Rookery marked the next big step forward in skyscraper construction. The Home Insurance Company Building had proved the strength and efficiency of the steel frame. Now the Rookery pointed the way toward a new type of foundation that would prevent tall, heavy office buildings from sinking into wet, sandy soil like that beneath Chicago.

Under the Rookery, Burnham and Root put footings made of steel railroad rails laid at right angles to the upright steel columns of the building and embedded in concrete. This "floating foundation" spread the weight of the building over a larger area than the bulky pyramids of stone and cement that had been used under the Home Insurance Company Building and other, earlier structures.

However, buildings with the new floating foundations still settled unevenly in Chicago's unstable soil. Sometimes one part of a building got as much as three or four inches out of line with another, and long cracks appeared in the walls. Only later, in the early 1900s, did builders devise ways to pump water out of the soil so that the footings, or piers, of skyscrapers could be extended down 75 or 100 feet (23–30.5 m) until they reached firm clay or bedrock. At the bottom of the piers of present-day skyscrapers, though, builders in Chicago and elsewhere still frequently put in floating foundations like those first used under the Rookery.

Two blocks east of the Rookery, a cluster of famous early skyscrapers is lined up along Dearborn Street. Although their ground floors have been remodeled over the years and their outside walls are sooty, these skyscrapers still have a certain majesty, and they continue to function as office buildings today.

Monadnock Block
(Hedrich Blessing)

One of them, the Monadnock Block, is the tallest skyscraper ever built entirely of masonry, without a steel frame. It was also one of the last. Designed by Burnham and Root, the architects of the Rookery, and completed in 1891, the Monadnock Block rose to an unprecedented height of 16 stories. To support that height, however, the masonry walls had to be six feet (1.8 m) thick at the base, and even at the top they were a foot and a half (45 cm) thick. Such thick walls were quite expensive to build and reduced the amount of rentable space, especially on the lower floors. The Monadnock Block helped to convince builders that future skyscrapers should be constructed with the new, light steel frames.

Still, the Monadnock Block was a forward-looking structure in other ways. To prevent the building from swaying in Chicago's high winds, the architects used a new form of reinforcement called "portal bracing." In this system, which was inspired by the bracing used in

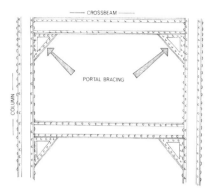

Detail of portal bracing in steel frame construction

early 19th-century bridges, triangular plates were riveted to the edges of both the vertical columns that supported the building's walls, and the horizontal beams that bore the weight of the floors. Portal bracing was later adapted to the needs of steel frame construction, and it helped lead to the development of taller and safer skyscrapers.

The design of the Monadnock Block was unusual, too. While most other office buildings of its day were heavily ornamented, the granite and brick walls of the Monadnock Block rose all the way up to the roof without a trace of decoration. The architects chose this clean, simple design because it made the building look even taller than it was.

Directly across Dearborn Street from the Monadnock Block stands a very different kind of early skyscraper, the 18-story Fisher Building, which was completed in 1896. While the Monadnock Block was one of the heaviest skyscrapers ever built, the Fisher Building was one of the lightest.

In order to reduce the load on its steel frame, the Fisher Building was covered not with stone or brick, but with lightweight panels of fired clay called terra cotta. Two-thirds of the building's surface was left to be filled in with windows, which caused one writer of the time to exclaim that it was "a building without walls!" Its window-covered surface makes the Fisher Building seem like the grandfather of all the glassy skyscrapers that dominate the skylines of our cities today.

The Fisher Building (Barbara Crane)

Not far from the skyscrapers along Dearborn Street stands one of Chicago's most famous cultural and architectural monuments, the Auditorium Building, completed in 1890. In 1975 this building was declared a National Historic Landmark by the United States Department of the Interior.

Although the Auditorium Building was not built as a skyscraper, its eight-story tower, rising above a huge auditorium seating 4,200 people, made it the tallest building in Chicago at the time of its construction. And it was designed by the man who probably contributed more to the development of the skyscraper than any other single architect: Louis Henri Sullivan.

Sullivan had come to work in Chicago after studying at the Massachusetts Institute of Technology and in Paris. A rebellious, poetic

The Auditorium Building (Barbara Crane)

Irishman, he believed in what he called "organic architecture." He thought the form of a building should reflect its function, and the materials of which it was made. If it was built on a steel frame, the architect shouldn't try to make it look as if it were constructed of masonry. If it was intended to be used as an office building, it shouldn't be designed to look like a medieval castle.

"What is the chief feature of an office building?" Sullivan asked in an article he wrote in 1896. "At once we answer, it is tall, it is lofty. It must be tall, every inch of it tall . . . it must be a proud and soaring thing, rising in sheer exultation from top to bottom without a single dissenting line."

Sullivan listed the five sections which he thought every office skyscraper should include:

1. A story or more below ground where the furnace and power equipment would be located.

2. An impressive ground floor with a grand main entrance and lobby, and space for stores, banks, and the like.

3. A mezzanine level of shops and offices above the ground floor, reached by stairs from the lobby. If the architect wished, part of the mezzanine could be left open to make the lobby even higher and more spacious.

4. As many office floors above the mezzanine level as the builder desired, all exactly alike, with sufficient light and air so that the workers in the offices would be comfortable.

5. An attic floor at the top containing machinery needed for elevators, the building's water supply, and other necessities.

Sullivan had a chance to test his theories of skyscraper construction in several tall office buildings he designed in the 1890s. Oddly enough, the two most famous Sullivan skyscrapers were not built in Chicago, but in other cities to which his fame had spread.

The ten-story Wainwright Building was completed in St. Louis in 1891. Red brick structures called piers rose from the third floor to the tenth, revealing the frame of the building and emphasizing its height. Around the front entrance and on the spaces, or spandrels, between the floors, Sullivan put the terra cotta panels for which he was famous. These featured leaf and flower patterns like the decorations in the lobby of his Auditorium Building in Chicago.

Even more striking, in the opinion of many architectural critics, was Sullivan's design for the 13-story Prudential Building, erected in Buffalo, New York, in 1894–95. It demonstrated the five-part form Sullivan believed every skyscraper should have. Above the basement was a pillared ground floor, and above that a mezzanine with large

The Wainwright Building. (Piaget, courtesy of the National Trust for Historic Preservation)

horizontal windows. Then came ten floors of offices framed by slender, soaring piers. Finally, at the top, there was an attic floor with round windows and heavily decorated cornice.

The combination of utility and beauty in the Wainwright and

Detail of a terra cotta panel on the Wainwright Building

Prudential buildings reflected Louis Sullivan's ideas of what a skyscraper should be. But many architects and builders didn't agree with his ideas. As America entered the 20th century, an entirely different approach to skyscraper design was taking shape in the East.

3 : THE SKYSCRAPER COMES TO NEW YORK

Louis Sullivan designed only one skyscraper in New York City, the 12-story Bayard Building, which was erected in 1898. Few visitors to New York are likely to see it, though. Hidden away on a narrow, shabby street, the Bayard Building is not one of the city's well-known skyscrapers. Nor are its clean, direct lines typical of the office towers that made New York's skyline famous.

The look of New York's early skyscrapers was partly determined by the physical nature of Manhattan Island. The city's solid rock base meant that heavy structures could be erected more easily than in the sandy soil of Chicago. And the long, narrow shape of Manhattan encouraged architects to build higher and higher in order to make the most of limited ground space.

Skyscraper design in New York was also influenced by the ambitions and desires of the people who financed the buildings. These real-estate developers, industrialists, and merchants wanted their names connected with magnificent-looking buildings that would proclaim their wealth and power to everyone who looked up at them.

New York architects in the early 1900s thought that the best way to satisfy their clients was to borrow design ideas for their skyscrapers from the temples of the ancient Greeks and Romans, and from the great Gothic cathedrals of Western Europe. Those structures had been built as monuments to emperors or gods; why not use them as models for skyscraper monuments to 20th-century millionaires?

This design approach was called the Beaux Arts style—which means "fine arts" in French—because many of the architects who used it had studied at the École des Beaux Arts in Paris. Whereas Louis Sullivan and other Chicago architects tried in many of their skyscrapers to reveal the steel framework beneath the stone or terra

The Bayard Building
(David Anderson)

cotta covering, Beaux Arts architects did their best to hide the framework under layers of elaborate decoration.

A good example of a Beaux Arts skyscraper is New York's Flatiron Building. Built as an office tower with shops on the ground floor, it was called the Fuller Building when it was completed in 1902.

But it soon acquired the nickname "Flatiron Building" because its triangular shape resembled the flatirons people used to press their clothing at the beginning of this century.

Interestingly, the Flatiron Building was designed by Daniel H. Burnham, the Chicago architect who, with John Wellborn Root, had designed both the Rookery and the Monadnock Block. After Root's death in 1891, Burnham's work had become less experimental and more conservative.

As in many other Beaux Arts skyscrapers, the 20 stories of the Flatiron Building are divided into three parts, like a classical Greek column. The first three floors, with their wide windows and rough

The Flatiron Building (David Anderson)

limestone covering, are the equivalent of a column's base. Then come 14 floors rising up and up like the shaft of a column.

Greek columns usually feature an ornate capital at the top, and so does the Flatiron Building. Its capital is formed by two upper floors decorated with arches and columns, followed by a final floor with windows that look like the portholes of a ship, and an elaborate cornice.

The gray limestone covering of the Flatiron Building is like that of an Italian palace from the Middle Ages, and the surface is heavily decorated. Looking up at the building from across the street can be like playing "Find What's Hidden in the Picture." At different heights

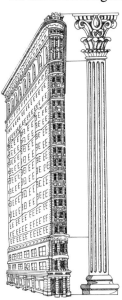

Comparison of the Flatiron Building and a classical Greek column

one can discover carved flowers, wreaths, the faces of Greek heroes, and the heads of lions. There couldn't be a sharper contrast with the clean, undecorated lines of the Monadnock Block and other Chicago skyscrapers.

Because of its triangular shape and prominent location, the Flatiron Building has attracted the notice of artists, writers, and photographers ever since it was built. Not everyone who saw the building liked it. The English artist Sir Philip Burne-Jones, who visited New

York in 1902, called it "a vast horror." However, the American journalist John Corbin admired its dramatic thrust and said it dominated the nearby avenues "like an ocean steamer with all Broadway in tow."

The French composer Camille Saint-Saëns thought the Flatiron Building made "a fantastic and marvelous spectacle." And the British author H. G. Wells expressed the feelings of many people, past and present, when he wrote in 1906, "I found myself agape, admiring a skyscraper—the prow of the Flatiron Building, to be particular, ploughing up through the traffic of Broadway and Fifth Avenue in the late afternoon light."

Automobiles and buses have replaced the horse-drawn carriages and streetcars that Wells saw. But the Flatiron Building still ploughs up through the traffic of the avenues today, and still commands the attention of countless visitors to New York City.

The Flatiron Building was only the first of a series of skyscrapers that rose higher and higher into the sky above New York in the first three decades of this century. Each one could claim—for a brief time—that it was the tallest building in the world.

The Singer Building on lower Broadway held the title for just one year, from 1908 until 1909. The ornate domed tower that topped its 47 stories of offices reached a height of 612 feet (187 m). Unfortunately, the Singer Building cannot be seen today; it was torn down in 1967 to make way for an even taller skyscraper.

The next winner in the tallest-building competition was the 700-foot (213 m) Metropolitan Life Insurance Company Tower, erected in 1909 along Madison Square Park, just a block away from the Flatiron Building. Its design was patterned on the famous bell tower in St. Mark's Square in Venice, but the 50-story Metropolitan Life Tower is more than twice as high as the tower in Venice.

The Metropolitan Life Tower boasts the largest four-faced clock in the world, located just below its roof. Each dial is 26½ feet (8 m) in diameter. The minute hands are 17 feet (5 m) long and weigh

The Metropolitan Life Tower
(David Anderson)

1,000 pounds (454 kg); the hour hands are 13 feet four inches (4 m) long and weigh 700 pounds (318 kg).

The beacon light atop the tower was christened "the light that never fails" at a Metropolitan Life convention in 1909. Since the building's opening, the light has shone continuously except during World War II, when dimout regulations required that it be shut off. It was relit on May 8, 1945, to help celebrate the Allied victory over Nazi Germany.

Beginning in 1909, thousands of people rode electric elevators up to the windswept observation deck on the 45th floor of the Metropolitan Life Tower. There they paid 50 cents—a lot of money in a time when many people made only ten dollars a week—to look out over the city and its suburbs and see "the homes of one-sixteenth of the population of the United States" (or so an advertisement claimed).

The Woolworth Building (David Anderson)

The tower deck remained open until 1917. By then New Yorkers and tourists were flocking to the observation floors of other skyscrapers, including the Woolworth Building, which in 1913 had replaced the Metropolitan Life Tower as the world's tallest building.

The 60-story Woolworth Building is named for Frank W. Woolworth, founder of the chain of stores that bear his name. Woolworth started his working life in 1873 as a store clerk in Watertown, New York, earning three dollars and 50 cents for a six-day, 84-hour week. In 1879, he opened his first successful five-cent store, and by 1911 he controlled more than 600 five-and-ten-cent stores in the United States, Canada, and England.

"After I was making a lot of money as a merchant," Woolworth once told a reporter, "I wanted to build something bigger than any other merchant ever had. The Woolworth Building is the result."

To design the building, Woolworth chose one of the most respected New York architects of the day, Cass Gilbert. Woolworth told Gilbert how much he admired the rich Gothic architecture of the Houses of Parliament in London, and said he wanted his building to be even more magnificent. Gilbert obliged him by decorating the tower of the Woolworth Building with Gothic arches, spires, flying buttresses, and gargoyles.

But Gilbert, influenced perhaps by Louis Sullivan's ideas about skyscrapers, also incorporated strong, clean piers in his design. These rise up from the main mass of the structure to the tall tower above, and on up to the Gothic spires at the summit, revealing the steel skeleton of the building and emphasizing its great height.

The Woolworth Building cost 13.5 million dollars to construct, and Frank W. Woolworth paid for it all in cash, out of his own fortune.

Nowhere is the grandeur of the Woolworth Building more evident than in the ground floor lobby. Walking into it is like entering a Moorish palace or a great cathedral. In fact, a prominent clergyman once described the building as a "Cathedral of Commerce." The walls are of beige marble from the Greek island of Skyros, and the arched

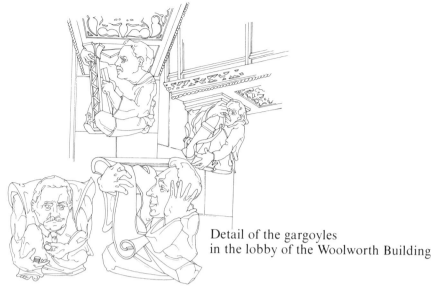

Detail of the gargoyles in the lobby of the Woolworth Building

ceiling, two stories high, is covered with blue, green, and gold mosaic tiles arranged in flower and bird designs. Above the elevator doors are glittering golden arches, and at the end of the lobby a grand marble stairway rises to the mezzanine.

Amid all this extravagance are some surprising touches of humor. Under the ornate ceiling beams in the lobby, the architect placed small gargoylelike figures. These are not dragons or other mythical creatures like the gargoyles that decorate Gothic cathedrals. Instead, they are caricatures of some of the people involved in the construction of the Woolworth Building. One is measuring a girder, another is checking figures on a long sheet of paper, others are watching a ticker tape. In one corner, Frank W. Woolworth himself can be seen counting the nickels and dimes that made him a millionaire—and enabled him to build the Woolworth Building.

The great height and weight of the Woolworth Building created many problems for the architects and engineers before and during construction, some of which were resolved as follows:

In order to give the structure a sturdy foundation, the builders sank metal tubes as large as 19 feet (5.75 m) in diameter down through soil, mud, silt, and water all the way to bedrock. They forced water

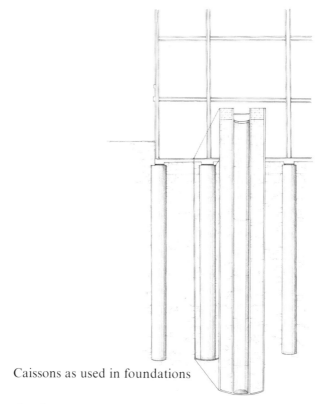
Caissons as used in foundations

and dirt out of the tubes by pneumatic pressure, and then filled them with concrete, forming 69 concrete piers called caissons upon which the steel columns of the building could rest.

For protection against the stresses of high winds, the tower of the Woolworth Building was constructed with portal braces much like those at the ends of bridges, and those in some of the first Chicago skyscrapers. Engineers claimed that even hurricane winds of 200 miles (320 km) an hour would not rock the Woolworth tower.

The building's copper roofs were connected by copper cables to the structural steelwork. Like a giant lightning rod, this served to ground the building and prevent lightning from damaging the structure.

The elevator system was the newest and finest in the world at the time the building was erected. There were 30 high-speed electric elevators in all, equipped with all the latest safety devices, including air cushioning in the shafts. Air cushioning allowed an elevator to land safely and smoothly on its own built-up air pressure even if all other safety devices failed.

To test the air-cushioning system, its inventor, F. T. Ellithorpe, loaded an elevator car with 7,000 pounds (3,175 kg) of ballast and a glass of water, and sent it plummeting from the 45th floor to the bottom of the elevator shaft, 600 feet (183 m) below. When the car came to rest, Ellithorpe proudly reported that not a single drop of water had been spilled from the glass.

To celebrate the completion of his building, Frank W. Woolworth gave a grand dinner on the evening of April 24, 1913, for over 800 guests. The dinner was held on the 27th floor of the skyscraper, and promptly at 7:30 all the lights in the banquet hall dimmed. Then a Western Union operator flashed a signal to the White House, where President Woodrow Wilson was waiting to press a button that would light the tallest building in the world with over 80,000 electric bulbs.

"A second later," the *New York American* reported the next day, "waiting thousands in New York and its suburbs saw, flashing in outlines of electric light, the greatest mountain of steel and stone ever erected by man—the gigantic Woolworth Building."

As they left work one evening and saw the lights of the building against the sky, one cleaning woman is said to have asked another, "How is it any man could build a buildin' like that?"

"That's easy to explain," her friend replied. "He did it with your ten cents and my ten cents."

Frank W. Woolworth watched over the new building from his private office on the 24th floor. Woolworth had modeled the office on the Empire Room of Napoleon's palace at Compiègne, France. The chairs were copies of the French ruler's throne, and the room's decorations included a life-size bust of Napoleon. Some journalists, after seeing the office, nicknamed Woolworth "the Napoleon of the dime stores."

Woolworth wasn't destined to enjoy his building for long. He died just six years after it was completed, in April, 1919. However, millions of Americans and tourists from abroad have been awed by the height and grandeur of the Woolworth Building in the years since. The 58th-floor observation gallery drew over 300,000 visitors a year all during the 1920s.

For almost 20 years the Woolworth Building remained the tallest building in the world, and today it is still among the top 25. It has been named an official landmark of New York City, and recently the Woolworth Company spent almost as much as the building originally cost to have its white terra cotta facade strengthened and restored.

This restoration will help to guarantee the future life of one of America's and the world's modern architectural monuments—a building that many still consider to be the most beautiful of all skyscrapers.

4 : THE SKYSCRAPER SPREADS ACROSS AMERICA

After World War I ended in 1918, the American economy boomed. As the nation entered the 1920s, agriculture became more mechanized. Fewer men were needed on the farms, so people flocked to the cities to find work in factories and offices.

Out of civic pride and because they needed more office space, cities large and small wanted their own equivalents of the Woolworth Building and the Metropolitan Life Tower. Soon skyscrapers began to rise all across America, from the Atlantic to the Pacific.

San Francisco's first skyscraper, the 18-story Standard Oil Building, erected in 1921, featured Gothic ornamentation like that of the Woolworth Building. The 31-story Russ Building, completed in San Francisco in 1927, also had Gothic elements—on either side of the main entrance were large niches like those in Gothic cathedrals. But while cathedral niches usually contained statues of saints, those on the Russ Building were simply for decoration, and were left empty.

By comparison with the 60-story Woolworth Building, 18- and 31-story skyscrapers wouldn't seem very tall, but in California they stood out like giants. Because of the threat of earthquakes, and the fear of what would happen if tall buildings toppled, many California cities, including Los Angeles, limited the height of office buildings to 150 feet (46 m) or 13 stories until well after World War II.

Back east, the Gothic influence could be seen in many other skyscrapers built during the 1920s. One of the most unusual was the so-called "Cathedral of Learning," erected by the University of Pittsburgh in 1926–27. Faced with increasing enrollment and limited space, university officials decided the only way to expand their facilities was to build upward. Steelmaker Andrew W. Mellon donated the land for the 42-story skyscraper, constructed in the Gothic style at a cost of 32 million dollars and containing college classrooms instead of

The Cathedral of Learning
(Ray Cristina,
courtesy of the University
of Pittsburgh News & Publications)

offices. Today the Cathedral of Learning is still recognized as the tallest educational structure ever built.

Probably the most Gothic-looking of all 1920s skyscrapers was the Tribune Tower, completed in Chicago in 1925. The design for the Tribune Tower was the result of an international architectural competition. In 1922, the *Chicago Tribune* announced that it would pay $100,000 in prize money to the architects who submitted the best designs for "the most beautiful office building in the world." First prize would be $50,000.

The *Tribune* received 285 submissions, 170 from America and 115 from 22 foreign countries. Some entries were jokes, like the one for a building topped by the figure of an American Indian, with a

Comic design submission for international architectural competition for the Tribune Tower

ceremonial war bonnet on his head and a tomahawk in his hand. But most were serious designs for handsome, functional skyscrapers. By unanimous vote of the jury, the first prize was awarded to Raymond M. Hood and John Mead Howells, architectural partners from New York. Their winning design in the Gothic style was inspired by the famous medieval Butter Tower in Rouen, France.

If the Woolworth Building is known as the "Cathedral of Commerce" and the University of Pittsburgh skyscraper as the "Cathedral of Learning," the Tribune Tower might be called the "Cathedral of Journalism." Its entrance arch, rich with stone carvings, reaches up three stories from the sidewalk, and its 36 floors are crowned with spires and huge flying buttresses. Raymond Hood wrote that he included the buttresses—which serve no practical purpose—so that the structure would seem to "soar magnificently into space."

More than 120 stones from every state in the union and famous places all over the world are embedded in the outer walls of the Tribune Tower. Some were put in place when the tower was first built; others have been obtained and inserted in the years since. There are stones from the White House, the Alamo in Texas, the Great Wall of China, the Colosseum in Rome, and from Adolf Hitler's bombed-out Reichschancellery in Berlin.

Not everyone agreed that Hood's and Howells' design for the Tribune Tower was the best one submitted. Critics pointed out that the Gothic decoration had nothing to do with either the steel frame construction of the building or its purpose as the home of a newspaper. They preferred the second-place design of Finnish architect Eliel Saarinen, with its strong vertical lines that revealed the steel skeleton beneath.

Louis Sullivan, the pioneer Chicago architect who was then nearing the end of his career and his life, was one of the most outspoken critics of Hood's and Howells' design, and a strong supporter of Saarinen's. Sullivan wrote, "Confronted by analysis, the first-prize design tumbles and falls crumbling to the ground. It is not architecture . . . its formula is literary. Next to the design of the Finn [Saarinen] it is a mere foundling."

Later developments seemed to prove that Sullivan and the other critics of the Tribune Tower were right. The Tribune Tower was one of the last great skyscrapers to be built in the Gothic style, while the clean lines and undecorated surfaces of Saarinen's second-place plans were widely copied in the following years.

However, anyone who sees the Tribune Tower by day on its impressive site just north of the Chicago River, or marvels at its flying buttresses, dramatically lit at night, can easily imagine why Hood's and Howells' design won first prize. For the Tribune Tower is still a strikingly handsome building.

While the Tribune Tower was under construction in Chicago, architects in New York were designing skyscrapers with a very different look. The shape of their buildings was determined by the New York City zoning law of 1916. Fearing that skyscrapers built straight up in the Gothic style would prevent light and air from reaching the streets below, New York City officials decreed that the upper stories of new office buildings must become progressively smaller, via setbacks,

Hugh Ferriss study for setback design (Scott Hyde, courtesy of Cooper-Hewitt Museum, Smithsonian Institution)

as the buildings reached higher into the sky. The number of setbacks depended on the width of the street—the narrower the street, the more setbacks there had to be—and a straight-rising tower was permitted on only part of the building site.

Modified versions of this zoning law spread from New York to other American cities during the 1920s and led to a new type of skyscraper—buildings that rose in steps like Mayan temples and were topped with one or more towers.

There was no single name for these new skyscrapers. Sometimes they were called "cubistic," after the style of painting popularized by Pablo Picasso and other artists; sometimes "Art Deco," from the design ideas introduced at the 1925 International Exposition of Decorative Arts in Paris; and sometimes simply "modernistic."

Art Deco skyscrapers were characterized by their ornament as well as their shape. Bands of brick, terra cotta, or metal in stylized floral designs or geometric patterns replaced the Gothic trim of earlier skyscrapers. The piers in Art Deco skyscrapers were usually bare of ornament and rose unbroken to the roofline, while the areas above and below windows were often clad in bricks or metal of a contrasting color to the piers. Art Deco decoration was meant to entertain and draw in the public, and to be good advertising for the business firms that occupied the skyscrapers.

One of the earliest and best examples of an Art Deco skyscraper is the 32-story Barclay–Vesey Building, designed by the architectural team of Voorhees, Gmelin, and Walker, and completed in New York City in 1926. Located between Barclay and Vesey Streets in downtown Manhattan, it was built to serve as an office and equipment center for the New York Telephone Company.

Because of its site, the Barclay–Vesey Building has an unusual form. The block on which it was built is parallelogram-shaped, and

The Barclay-Vesey Building
(David Anderson)

so are the lower floors of the skyscraper. Above this base, through a series of dramatic setbacks that conform to the 1916 zoning law, rises a rectangular tower inspired by the strong lines of Eliel Saarinen's second-place design for the Tribune Tower.

Over the entrances and at the tops of the setbacks, the Barclay–Vesey Building sports a rich assortment of Art Deco decoration. Fruit, animals, and human figures appear, carved in low relief in stone, and similar decorations are repeated on the lobby walls and on the doors of the elevators. Writing soon after the Barclay–Vesey Building opened, architectural critic Lewis Mumford said that it "expresses the achievements of contemporary American architecture better than any other skyscraper I have seen."

Another outstanding Art Deco skyscraper is the 45-story Chicago Board of Trade Building, which opened in 1930. Its 36-story tower is set back from the nine-story base, and is flanked by two wings

Left: the Los Angeles City Hall (courtesy of Albert C. Martin & Associates);
right: the Union Terminal Tower (courtesy of the Western Reserve Historical Society)

that rise 13 stories on either side of it. The gray limestone piers of the tower climb straight to the roofline in order to emphasize the building's height. Because grain is one of the chief commodities traded in the building, the pyramid-shaped roof is crowned with a modernistic aluminum statue of Ceres, Roman goddess of grain and the harvest.

The stepped-back look also characterizes the City Hall of Los Angeles, California, completed in 1929. Its four-story, block-square base features great entrance arches in the Spanish style of old California architecture. Above the base rises a 28-story tower with wings on either side. The tower, which reaches a height of 454 feet (138 m) above street level, made the City Hall the tallest building in Los Angeles until 1966, when the 42-story 500-foot-high Union Bank Building was completed. The carefully braced frame of the City Hall enabled it to resist the severe earthquake of 1933 and other, later quakes.

A pioneer grouping of tall buildings, all pointing toward a central skyscraper, was erected in Cleveland, Ohio, in the late 1920s. Three separate buildings, the 12-story Higbee Company department store, the 18-story Medical Arts Building, and the 12-story Hotel Cleveland, rose like the setbacks of a single huge skyscraper around the 52-story

Union Terminal Tower. At 708 feet (216 m), the Union Terminal Tower was known as the tallest building in the world outside New York City from 1929, when it opened, until 1967, when the John Hancock Building in Chicago surpassed it.

The Union Terminal complex was built by two shy brothers, Oris and Mantis Van Sweringen, who worked their way up from impoverished boyhoods to become two of the richest and most powerful men in America. By the end of the 1920s, they had large holdings in real estate, including the Cleveland suburb of Shaker Heights, which they had developed, and were also the owners of six major railroads. Their railroad investments alone were said to be worth between three and four billion dollars.

Like Frank W. Woolworth with his Woolworth Building, the Van Sweringens wanted the Union Terminal complex to serve not only as a terminal for the railroads they owned, but also as a monument to their wealth and power. "Do it right," Oris Van Sweringen said to one of the project's engineers, "and don't worry about the money."

Thirty-five acres in downtown Cleveland were cleared to make way for the Union Terminal complex, and 15,000 people had to find new homes elsewhere. Some of the 1,400 buildings that were torn down were rat-infested slums, but others were historic structures from the city's past that could never be replaced. Starting in 1923, three million cubic yards (2.3 million cubic meters) of earth were excavated for the project in what was described as "the greatest peacetime engineering feat since the digging of the Panama Canal."

Because of its vast scope, and because safety precautions were often ignored, working on the Union Terminal project could be dangerous—even fatal. Two "sandhogs," men who remove stones and earth from deep foundation shafts, died when 50 tons (45,000 kg) of liquid cement broke through the dirt wall of the shaft they were clearing and buried them. Other workers were killed when they fell from the steel girders of the tower, on which men labored even in rain and snow. At last the State of Ohio sent a team of officials to inspect the project, and they halted construction until all the building equipment was made safe.

On August 19, 1927, two workers raised the American flag high above the Terminal Tower to signal that its highest point had been reached. The first train entered the still-unfinished station on December 1, 1929, and on June 28, 1930, a dedication dinner was held in the great arrival and departure hall of the terminal. More than 2,500 industrial and civic leaders from all over the country gathered to celebrate the occasion while floodlights shone on the tower and giant searchlights at the top probed the night sky. Some said the searchlights could be seen as far away as Canada, 55 miles (89 km) away across Lake Erie.

Two prominent local people who failed to attend the celebration were the Van Sweringen brothers themselves. Too shy to face the crowd, they listened to a radio report of the ceremony from the privacy of their country home.

The Van Sweringens lost most of their money and died during the Great Depression of the 1930s, and with the decline of railroading in recent years, few trains use the terminal anymore. The grand concourse where the celebration dinner was held in 1930 is now an indoor tennis court.

However, the Union Terminal complex of buildings still plays an active, vital role in the business life of Cleveland. And the tower itself still lends drama, beauty, and grandeur to the Cleveland skyline, even though it is no longer the tallest skyscraper in the world outside New York City.

5: THE CHRYSLER BUILDING AND THE EMPIRE STATE BUILDING

As more and more skyscrapers were built, more and more people crowded into city centers to work and to shop, and traffic became extremely congested.

In 1923, Harvey Wiley Corbett, a professor of architecture at Columbia University, proposed a solution to the traffic problem in New York City. He suggested that pedestrians walk along second-story sidewalks, cantilevered out from the walls of tall buildings, and cross streets on bridges at the corners. Meanwhile, as many as 20 lanes of traffic would roar through the broad streets and avenues below.

Corbett's suggestions were never followed, and people continued to build new skyscrapers, despite the problems they created. By the end of the 1920s, American cities boasted 377 skyscrapers of more than 20 stories, 188 of which were in New York City. Of those 188, 15 were over 500 feet (152 m) tall. And one of them, the 77-story Chrysler Building, finally challenged the Woolworth Building for the title of tallest building in the world. The steel spire atop the Chrysler Building reached the unprecedented height of 1,048 feet (319 m).

Many consider the Chrysler Building to be the most striking of all the Art Deco skyscrapers built in the 1920s. On a sunny day its stainless steel surface makes the building visible from miles away, and its rich ornamentation is a delight to study. To promote the fact that the building was erected by the Chrysler Motors Corporation, the walls were decorated with bands of brickwork in the form of automobile hubcaps, and gargoyles modeled on radiator ornaments were placed around the upper floors. Six levels of curving metal arches with triangular windows set in them make the tower look like a stainless steel rainbow, or the crown of the Statue of Liberty.

More than almost any other skyscraper, the Chrysler Building reflected the energy, optimism, and zest for living that characterized

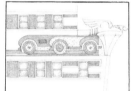

Above: detail of ornamental brickwork on the Chrysler Building; *left:* the Chrysler Building (David Anderson)

the 1920s. However, its reign as the tallest building in the world was destined to last only a few months. For even as the Chrysler Building celebrated its official opening in 1930, the foundation was being laid for the next world champion—the Empire State Building.

Today, the Empire State Building symbolizes New York City for many people, but it almost didn't get built.

Plans for the building were first announced in August, 1929, just

 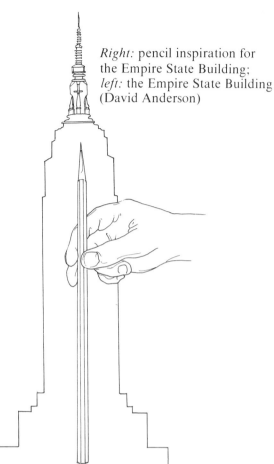

Right: pencil inspiration for the Empire State Building; *left:* the Empire State Building (David Anderson)

two months before the stock market crash that led to the Great Depression of the 1930s. The new skyscraper was to be 80 stories high and was to cost 60 million dollars. After the crash, some doubted that the necessary funds for the building could be raised. But in December, 1929, the Metropolitan Life Insurance Company came through with a loan of 27 million dollars, and the project got under way.

Unlike the Woolworth Building and the Union Terminal complex in Cleveland, the Empire State Building was not the dream of one or two wealthy individuals, but rather the idea of a group of businessmen who wanted to build a beautiful building—the tallest in the world—but were also concerned that it be done as quickly, economically, and efficiently as possible. William F. Lamb, the architect of the Empire State Building, described the program he was given by the building's developers: "It was short enough—a fixed budget, as many stories and as much office space as possible, an exterior of limestone, and completion by May, 1931, which meant only a year and six months from the beginning of sketches."

According to Lamb's widow, a pencil was his original inspiration for the building's design. One day he stood an eraser-less pencil on end, with its point in the air, and sketched it. That was only his first rough sketch, however; Lamb later revised his drawings for the building 16 times.

The final approved design featured a five-story base from which an 81-story tower would rise in a series of setbacks in order to meet New York City's zoning requirements. The upper part of the tower, above the setbacks, would occupy only half an acre of the two-acre site at Fifth Avenue and 34th Street.

Excavation on the foundation started in late January, 1930. Footings for 210 steel and concrete columns were driven down to bedrock, which was about 33 feet (10 m) below sidewalk level. The columns and the bedrock beneath them had to be strong enough to support the 303,000 tons (273 million kg) of steel, stone, and other materials that would go into the Empire State Building.

Work on the steel skeleton of the building began on St. Patrick's Day, March 17, 1930. Fifty-seven thousand tons (51 million kg) of steel were needed for the skeleton, enough to build a double-track railroad between New York City and Baltimore, Maryland, 198 miles (319 km) away.

The steel for the frame was poured and set into girders in the steel mills of Pittsburgh. The girders then were shipped by freight train to a waterfront supply yard in New Jersey, and trucked from there to the Fifth Avenue building site. Raising gangs hoisted the girders in bundles to riveting gangs working at the top of the structure. A sticker-in put each girder in place, and two riveters secured it with noisy pneumatic riveting hammers. At the peak of construction, 38 gangs of riveters were at work high atop the frame.

A photographer named Lewis W. Hine took many photographs of the steelworkers in action. In order to get photos of riveters working at the very top of the tower, 1,000 feet (305 m) above the street, Hine was swung out from the frame in a specially designed basket.

The steel skeleton of the Empire State Building was completed in just 23 weeks. However, the rapid pace of construction cost the lives of 14 workers; they died as a result of falls and other accidents.

After the frame was in place, derrick slings lifted large slabs of limestone to the upper floors, and workers began to enclose the building. More than 3,000 bricklayers, carpenters, electricians, plumbers, elevator installers, and other workers labored daily on the project. Cement for the building came from upstate New York, limestone from quarries in Indiana, lumber from the Pacific Coast, hardware from factories in New England, and marble from France and Italy.

So the workers would not have to leave their work sites for lunch, mobile cafeterias shuttled up and down the scaffolding from floor to floor at noontime. Miles of temporary pipes provided drinking water. A small hospital, equipped with a staff of nurses and doctors and an emergency operating room, was opened in the base of the building.

As the building rose higher, miniature railroad cars were installed on each floor to carry supplies from one end to the other. Every morning the car operators received timetables of the shipments of steel beams, bricks, window frames, and other materials that would be coming up during the day, and instructions on when and where to deliver them. As a result, most workers never had to wait for the materials they needed, and were able to accomplish more in a shorter time.

The Empire State Building was completed ahead of schedule on April 11, 1931, and still holds the world record for the fastest-rising skyscraper ever built. The official opening ceremony took place on May 1, 1931. Following the pattern established when President Woodrow Wilson lit the Woolworth Building for the first time, President

Opposite: construction of the Empire State Building (courtesy of the International Museum of Photography at George Eastman House, Lewis Hine, photographer)

Artist's rendition of a dirigible
attempting to moor atop the Empire State Building

Herbert Hoover pushed a button in Washington to light the handsome marble lobby of the Empire State Building.

After the ceremony, a buffet luncheon was served on the 86th floor to the distinguished guests, among whom was Franklin D. Roosevelt, then the governor of New York. From the observation deck the guests could look up at the 200-foot-high (61 m) mooring mast that had been placed at the very top of the building's tower.

The mast had been designed as a landing for dirigibles, the giant airships that were then the latest thing in air travel. If all had gone according to plan, transatlantic dirigibles would have flown up Manhattan Island and hooked onto the mooring mast atop the Empire State Building. An enclosed gangplank would have been lowered from the airship, and the passengers would have walked down it to a platform at the top of the building. From the platform express elevators would have whisked them down to the street.

Engineers warned that airships would swing too much in the wind for the mooring mast to work safely. But it was built in spite of the warnings, and two landings were attempted after the Empire State Building was completed.

On September 15, 1931, a privately owned dirigible tied up to the mast, but stayed only three minutes because a 45-mile-an-hour (72 kph) wind was whipping the airship. Two weeks later, a Navy dirigible landed long enough to deliver some papers to the building. However, an updraft of air almost upended the ship, and when the crew dumped water ballast from the craft in a frantic attempt to steady it, pedestrians in the streets below were soaked.

No passenger dirigible ever tied up to the mast, and dirigible travel itself went out of style after the German airship *Hindenburg* burst into flame, killing all on board, while attempting to land at Lakehurst, New Jersey, in 1937. Eventually the landing platform was transformed into a second, higher observation deck on what became the 102nd story of the Empire State Building.

Soon after the building opened, its architects were awarded a gold medal by the New York Architectural League, and in 1932 the New York chapter of the American Institute of Architects gave them its medal of honor, saying, "In the monumental design of a great office building, they have made a genuine contribution to architecture." But because of poor business conditions caused by the Depression, less than 30 percent of the offices in the building were rented. Some said it should be renamed the "Empty State Building."

What kept the building going were the flocks of sightseers who came to see it. On the first day it was open to the public in 1931, over 5,000 people roamed through it, and within a month 100,000 more had paid a dollar apiece—a large sum in those days—to ride the elevators up to the 86th floor observation deck.

Many famous people, from movie stars to sports figures to rulers of foreign countries, visited the Empire State Building when they were in New York. Countless others in the United States and abroad got their first glimpse of the building when Hollywood used it in 1933 as the setting for the climax of *King Kong*. The giant 50-foot (15-m) ape stood on top of the tower with a young woman clutched in one fist while he tried to fend off a squadron of Army fighter planes with the other.

The building withstood the attack of Kong in the movie, and it has endured even more damaging assaults in reality. Winds of as high as 110 miles (177 km) an hour have made the structure bend, but its elastic steel frame has kept it from swaying. In severe thunderstorms the building has been struck by as many as 200,000 amperes of electricity nine times in less than 20 minutes. Its steel frame has acted as a giant lightning rod, grounding even the most powerful bolts.

Probably the greatest threat to the Empire State Building came at 9:52 on a foggy Saturday morning in July, 1945, when a B-25 Army bomber, flying over New York at 1,000 feet (305 m) instead of the usual 2,000-foot (610-m) minimum, crashed into the north side of the building between the 78th and 79th floors. According to an observer, the noise of the crash sounded like an earthquake.

The impact sheared off the plane's wings, which fell to the roof of the fifth floor, 74 floors below. The plane roared on into the skyscraper, tearing a hole in the wall 18 feet (5.5 m) wide and 20 feet (6 m) high. Its gasoline tanks exploded, sending flames shooting up as high as the 86th observation deck, and turning the 78th and 79th floors into an inferno.

The plane's pilot, a crew member, and the single passenger all died in the flames, their bodies burned beyond recognition. Eleven office workers on the 79th floor were also burned to death. No doubt the toll would have been even higher if the accident had occurred on a weekday.

All ten elevators that served the observation deck were put out of commission. Luckily, there weren't many passengers in them that early in the morning, but more than an hour passed before some of the operators were rescued. Many people, including those on the observation deck, had to walk 70 or 80 stories down the stairs in order to get out of the building.

Fortunately, no permanent damage was done to the main structure of the Empire State Building. However, it took over a year and cost more than a million dollars to repair the elevators and the burned-out 78th and 79th floors.

Today thousands of tourists still visit the Empire State Building each year, even though it is no longer the tallest building in the world. Their first glimpse of the building, towering above its neighbors, is likely to make them catch their breath even though they've seen it many times in photographs. And once they've entered the impressive marble lobby and ridden one elevator to the 80th floor, then another to the 86th, and finally another, smaller one to the observatory on the 102nd floor, they may well gasp when they look at the views through the porthole-like windows. On a clear day they'll be able to see 80 miles (129 km) in any direction. Descending to the larger observation deck on the 86th floor, they can stroll around the outdoor terrace.

Since 1964, the top 30 floors of the Empire State Building have been floodlit at night throughout the year, except on overcast nights during the spring and fall when birds are migrating. On foggy nights birds are likely to fly toward brightly lit buildings and crash into them, killing themselves. Over 400 crashed into the Empire State Building on a single drizzly night in 1970, before the policy of turning off the floodlights was adopted.

In 1979 it was proposed that the Empire State Building be named an official landmark of New York City. Such a designation would mean that changes could not be made in the building without the approval of the city's Landmarks Preservation Commission, and would help to prevent its being altered or demolished at some future date.

But for countless people in the United States and abroad, the Empire State Building has been a landmark ever since it opened over 50 years ago. In fact, if asked for the name of the most famous skyscraper in the world, many would probably reply automatically, "The Empire State Building."

6 : A SKYSCRAPER CITY

In 1931, Raymond Hood, the architect of the Chicago Tribune Tower, published an article, "City Under a Single Roof," that attracted much attention. "The growth of cities is getting beyond control," Hood wrote. "Skyscrapers create congestion. Subways are built resulting in more skyscrapers, and so on in an ascending spiral. Where will it end? Here is the answer . . . related communities in the city."

Hood looked ahead to "Manhattan 1950," and imagined Manhattan Island dotted with 38 giant skyscraper clusters, each one a city within a city containing offices, apartments, stores, and places of amusement. Workers would live in the same skyscraper towers where their offices were located, and could easily walk to nearby shops and theaters. Auto traffic would be reduced, traffic jams eliminated, and the city would become a pleasanter and more comfortable place.

Hood didn't live to see how different the actual Manhattan of 1950 was from the city he envisioned. But he did have the chance to try out his ideas for a skyscraper city-within-a-city as a member of the team of architects that designed Rockefeller Center.

Like the Woolworth Building, Rockefeller Center is named for its principal financial backers. These were John D. Rockefeller, Jr., and other members of the wealthy Rockefeller family. Built in New York City between 1931 and 1940, with later skyscrapers added after World War II, Rockefeller Center now includes 18 buildings that cover 22 acres of midtown Manhattan and contain more than ten million square feet (929,000 square meters) of rentable space.

The best place to begin a tour of Rockefeller Center is on Fifth Avenue between 49th and 50th Streets. From there a flagstone promenade, nicknamed the Channel Gardens because it is between the six-story British Building to the north and the matching six-story French Building to the south, slopes gently downward into Rockefeller Center.

During the spring and summer, water splashes from fountainheads in the form of dolphins with human riders into six stepped-down ponds in the middle of the promenade. Around the ponds are plantings that reflect the changing seasons: Easter lilies in the spring, roses in the summer, chrysanthemums in the fall, and abstract metal angels blowing trumpets at Christmastime.

When you reach the foot of the Channel Gardens, a full story below Fifth Avenue, you will find yourself looking down into a great sunken plaza. At the far side of the plaza a bronze statue of the Greek god Prometheus, sculpted by Paul Manship and painted gold, seems to fly up out of a marble fountain. Prometheus was the god who stole fire from heaven and taught human beings how to use it for their benefit. The statue of Prometheus in the sunken plaza symbolizes human progress, which is the theme of all the artworks in Rockefeller Center, and of the center itself.

In summer diners enjoy eating under umbrellas in an outdoor café beside the Prometheus fountain, while in fall, winter, and spring the plaza is transformed into an outdoor ice-skating rink where thousands of skaters display their skill. Every year at Christmas a giant

Statue of Prometheus and the Christmas Tree above the skating rink in Rockefeller Center (David Anderson)

spruce tree, never less than 65 feet (20 m) tall and 30 feet (9 m) in diameter, is trucked down from the north woods and installed in the plaza above the Prometheus fountain. The tree is so tall that workmen have to put up scaffolding in order to decorate it. The tree's great size, its glittering lights, and its commanding position in the middle of Rockefeller Center have made it one of the most famous Christmas trees in the nation.

When you look up from the sunken plaza, you'll realize that you're standing at the heart of Rockefeller Center. Beyond the terraces that surround the plaza, bordered by rows of sycamore trees and poles from which the flags of the United Nations fly, you can see five great skyscrapers, all the same gray color, and all designed in the same clean-lined style.

To the south along Rockefeller Plaza, a street that was created especially for the center, stand the 16-story Eastern Airlines Building and, opposite it, the 36-story office tower that was the first Time-Life Building. To the north stand the 15-story Associated Press Building and the long 45-story slab of the International Building. Rising directly in front of you is the tallest and most impressive of all the skyscrapers in Rockefeller Center, the 70-story RCA (Radio Corporation of America) Building.

Slender and sleek, the RCA Building climbs through a series of setbacks to a height of 850 feet (259 m). It was one of the first skyscrapers to be equipped with high-speed elevators; they whiz upward at 1,400 feet (427 m) per minute. It was also one of the first great office towers to be air-conditioned in the summer.

On the 70th floor of the RCA Building there is an outdoor observation deck from which you can get a marvelous view of other New York skyscrapers, including the Empire State Building just 15 blocks to the south. Also located at the top of the building is the Rainbow Room and Grill, where people eat and dance while looking out at spectacular views of New York City at night.

Unlike the walls of the Woolworth Building and the Tribune Tower, the exterior walls of the RCA Building are almost totally

The RCA Building (David Anderson)

free of decoration. They were left bare partly to save money, and partly because the architects were influenced by clean-cut, modernistic designs like the one for the Barclay–Vesey Building. However, there are Art Deco–style ornaments sculpted in low relief around and above the entrances to the RCA Building, and dramatic murals on the black marble walls of the lobby.

The famous Mexican artist Diego Rivera was originally commissioned to paint the lobby murals for the RCA Building. But when Rivera, who held radical political views, included pictures of striking workers and Russians mourning at the tomb of Vladimir Lenin, the first Communist leader of the Soviet Union, the Rockefeller family became upset. Rivera's murals didn't seem appropriate for a project like Rockefeller Center, which was meant to be a monument to the American capitalistic system.

The Rockefellers paid off Rivera, had his murals erased from the walls, and hired the Spanish artist José Maria Sert to paint new ones in their place. Sert's murals feature gigantic human figures that look almost three-dimensional and embody Rockefeller Center's theme of progress. They portray the 19th-century philosopher Ralph Waldo Emerson and President Abraham Lincoln as examples of the thinkers and doers who contributed to the growth and development of the United States.

The entrances and lobbies of other Rockefeller Center skyscrapers also feature striking murals and works of art. The circular lobby of the Eastern Airlines Building boasts a mural by artist Dean Cornwell that shows the entire history of American transportation, from covered wagons crossing the plains to airplanes flying across the continent. In front of the Fifth Avenue entrance to the International Building, which houses many foreign airline and travel offices, there stands a huge statue by Lee Lawrie of the Greek god Atlas, bending under the weight of the world which he holds aloft in his muscular arms. The lobby of the International Building is a modern version of a Greek temple, with green marble columns reaching up two full stories to a glowing copper ceiling.

Under all the skyscrapers in Rockefeller Center, and linking them below ground, are concourses lined with restaurants and shops of all kinds. There are clothing stores, barbershops, travel agencies, photography studios, and even an underground post office. Corridors lead from the concourses to the subway and to parking garages for private cars. Each day over 250,000 people come to Rockefeller Center to shop, to work, or to see the sights.

Many also come to be entertained, for Rockefeller Center contains one of the largest and most famous theaters in the country—the 6,200-seat Radio City Music Hall. The Music Hall was opened in 1932 and quickly became known as "the showplace of the nation."

A visitor to the Music Hall can't help but be impressed by the lobby, 140 feet (42.5 m) long, 45 feet (14 m) wide, and 60 feet (18 m) tall, with Art Deco chandeliers hanging from the ceiling and a grand stairway leading up to the balcony past a dramatic mural of the fountain of youth. Inside the theater, under the high curved ceiling, an organ swings out from one wall, the entire orchestra can be raised from the pit, and the troupe of 35 young women known as the Rockettes performs complicated dance routines in perfect unison.

Since World War II, four more tall skyscrapers—the second Time-Life Building, the Exxon Building, the McGraw-Hill Building, and the Celanese Building—have been erected along Sixth Avenue across from Rockefeller Center. Considered part of the center, these commercial office buildings, with their flat tops and slablike walls, look almost like four armored giants lined up along Sixth Avenue.

In 1969, the American Institute of Architects honored the group of 14 buildings erected in Rockefeller Center between 1931 and 1940 by awarding it the Institute's Twenty-Five-Year Citation for Architectural Excellence. The citation read, in part:

> "To a lesson in land use which devotes such large areas to air and space, but also to human enjoyment.
>
> "To a group of high structures which offered a new approach to urban planning.
>
> "To a project so vital to the city and alive with its people that it remains as viable today as when it was built."

Rockefeller Center has been the inspiration for other skyscraper cities in the United States, from Peachtree Center in Atlanta, to the Galleria complex in Houston, to Century City in Los Angeles, and Embarcadero Center in San Francisco. But none has yet achieved the unique blend of shops, theaters, open spaces, and soaring office towers that makes Rockefeller Center so satisfying.

7 : GLASS BOXES AROUND THE WORLD

After Rockefeller Center was completed, few new skyscrapers were built anywhere in the world until after World War II ended in 1945. First, the Depression of the 1930s reduced the amount of money available for new construction projects. Then, during the war, the steel and other materials that go into skyscrapers were needed for the manufacture of tanks, guns, and fighter planes.

Before the war, there were few skyscrapers in the old cities of Europe and Asia. But during the war the central districts of such cities as London, Berlin, and Moscow were heavily damaged in bombing raids. Afterward skyscrapers rose in many of these bombed-out districts just as they had risen for the first time in Chicago after the Great Fire of 1871.

In Moscow between 1949 and 1953, Joseph Stalin, then the ruler of the Soviet Union, ordered the construction of seven widely spaced Gothic skyscrapers as a monument to the nation's wartime victory over Nazi Germany. Because the word "skyscraper" was so closely associated with the cities of the capitalistic Western world that Stalin hated, he decreed that the new Moscow towers be called "multistory buildings" instead.

The tallest of the Moscow skyscrapers is the main building of Moscow State University, located on the Lenin Hills to the west of the city. Its 32-story main tower rises to a height of 1,247 feet (380 meters) and is crowned with a golden star set in ears of wheat. Lower blocks of 12 and 18 stories, each with turrets of its own, flank the main tower, and 328 feet (100 meters) above the entrance are statues of a male worker and a collective-farm woman, symbolizing the people of the Soviet Union.

Most postwar skyscrapers were not built in the ornate Gothic style of Moscow's "multistory buildings." A new approach to sky-

Moscow State University
(*Tass*, courtesy of Sovfoto)

scraper design called the International Style had come to the fore. Skyscrapers built in this style had a sleek, streamlined appearance that suited the longing of people in the postwar world for the new and the modern.

The father of the International Style was the German architect Ludwig Mies van der Rohe. Mies was born in 1886 in the ancient town of Aachen, which had been founded in the ninth century by the great emperor Charlemagne. Many buildings from the Middle Ages still remained in Aachen when Mies was growing up, and years later he described how they had looked to him. "Those buildings were mostly simple but very clear," he said. "They had been standing there for over a thousand years and were still impressive."

Mies' father was a stonecutter, and the boy often helped in the family stonecutting shop. This experience gave him a working knowledge of basic building materials and a lifelong respect for them.

As a young man Mies went to Berlin, where he studied and worked with the well-known architect Peter Behrens. Behrens' clean-lined designs for industrial buildings made a strong impression on him. During World War I, Mies served in the German army as an engineer, and after the war was over he opened an architectural office of his own in Berlin.

Between 1919 and 1921 Mies drew sketches for two skyscrapers unlike any that had been conceived before. One tower was 20 stories high, the other 30, and both were to be covered entirely with glass. Although neither project was ever actually built, Mies' drawings were published in many countries and brought him immediate attention. As Peter Blake said in his biography of Mies, "With a few strokes of his pen, as it were, Mies laid the foundation for all the great steel-and-glass skyscrapers we see around us today."

Mies became famous for his sayings as well as for his skyscraper designs. Especially well-known is the answer he gave to an interviewer who wondered why there were virtually no ornaments on his skyscrapers. "Because less is more," Mies said.

In 1930 Mies was appointed to be the director of the Bauhaus school in Dessau, Germany. Bauhaus means "house of building," and the aim of the school was to coordinate advances in 20th-century technology with designs for buildings, furniture, fabrics, and even paintings. By the time Mies arrived at the Bauhaus, the school had become one of the outstanding centers of modern design and architecture in the world.

Despite its reputation, the Bauhaus had some dangerous enemies. The Nazis, who were rising to power in Germany at the time, called its designs "un-German," and forced the school to close in Dessau. Mies reopened it in Berlin, but closed it for good in 1933 in the face of new threats from the Nazis after Adolf Hitler became the leader of Germany.

Mies stayed on in Germany until 1937, when he was invited to come to the United States and was offered a job as director of architecture at the Illinois Institute of Technology in Chicago. From then until the end of his life he lived and worked in the United States.

Although Mies' architectural ideas were new to many of his students, they were not completely unknown in America. In 1932, while Mies was still directing the Bauhaus School in Dessau, Henry-Russell Hitchcock and Philip Johnson, who was later to become an architect himself, organized an exhibit of modern architecture at the Museum of Modern Art in New York. The exhibit included many of Mies' designs. Hitchcock and Johnson were the ones who christened the new trend in architecture "the International Style," and later they wrote an influential book about it.

A few pioneer skyscrapers in the International Style were designed and built during the 1930s. One was the Philadelphia Saving Fund Society Building, erected in Philadelphia in 1932. Its vertical lines and ribbonlike windows embodied many of the ideas put forth by the Bauhaus school.

Another early International Style skyscraper was the Ministry of Education and Health Building in Rio de Janeiro. It was designed by the famous Swiss-born architect Le Corbusier in 1936. Set on stilts called *pilotis,* Le Corbusier's flat-roofed skyscraper was 17 stories high and had narrow, blank end walls and long side walls covered with windows.

It wasn't until 1949, however, that Mies himself finally got the opportunity to build the sort of steel-and-glass skyscrapers he had first visualized back in 1919. A real-estate developer commissioned him to design two 26-story apartment towers overlooking Lake Michigan on Lake Shore Drive in Chicago.

Mies set the two flat-topped buildings a short distance apart, with their long sides at right angles to each other. The lobbies were enclosed in 17-foot-high (5-m) walls of glass, and all the apartments had floor-to-ceiling windows. When the buildings first opened, a reporter for the *Chicago Tribune* wrote, "Now people really *do* live in glass houses."

A Chicago building regulation said that all steel-framed buildings had to be fireproofed with two inches of concrete around the structural steel columns and the steel mullions between the windows. Mies didn't want the concrete coverings to show, so he decided to cover them in turn with black steel plate onto which he welded eight inch (20-cm) I beams at right angles. The I beams emphasized the height of the two buildings and created attractive patterns of light and shadow.

Walter Peterhans, who taught with Mies at the Illinois Institute of Technology, wrote soon after the Lake Shore Drive apartment buildings were completed, "These towers are built out of the familiar materi-

als, steel and glass, and yet it is as if steel and glass are seen for the first time."

Left: Mies van der Rohe's Lake Shore Drive Apartments (New York Public Library); *right:* the Lever House

As it turned out, Mies' glass-covered apartment towers were perfectly timed. In the postwar years it had become too expensive to cover skyscrapers with terra cotta, and rising labor costs made masonry construction uneconomical, too. Glass seemed the ideal solution to the problem. Readily available, it was thin yet sturdy, it could be made weatherproof and vaporproof, and it could be installed in large precut panels. Within a few years, glass-covered skyscrapers were rising in cities all over the United States.

Outstanding examples in New York City include the 39-story United Nations Secretariat Building along the East River, with its green-tinted walls of glass that reflect clouds and sunsets and other

Manhattan skyscrapers, and the 24-story office tower of Lever House, which looks almost like two glistening bars of green soap, one lying flat and the other standing on end. This is appropriate, since Lever Brothers manufactures Palmolive Soap and other soap products.

Probably the most striking of all the glass skyscrapers built in the 1950s is another designed by Mies: the 38-story Seagram Building, erected on Park Avenue in New York in 1958. Mies wanted passersby to experience the full height of the Seagram Building, so he set it back almost 100 feet (30.5 m) from the avenue on a granite-paved plaza. There are long, fountain-filled pools on both sides of the plaza, with small groves of gingko trees growing behind them. The tower itself is raised on stilts like Mies' Lake Shore Drive apartment buildings, but unlike them its columns, mullions, and spandrels are covered with bronze, not steel. The glass of the windows is tinted brown to match the bronze.

With its strong vertical lines and lack of decoration, the Seagram Building has a look of simplicity. But great attention was paid to every detail of its construction and furnishing. All signs, doorknobs, mail chutes, faucets, and even toilet seats were carefully designed to make the building a unified whole. Because of this, the Seagram Building was probably the most expensive skyscraper, per square foot, that had ever been erected up to that time.

During the late 1950s and the 1960s, office towers in the style of the Seagram Building sprang up in cities all over the world, from Buenos Aires to Capetown to Hong Kong. They could be built quickly and quite cheaply if standard designs were followed and less expensive materials than those in the Seagram Building were used.

Such skyscrapers filled the need for more office space and created a skyline for smaller cities that had never had one before. However, when three or more of these buildings were grouped together, their sameness and lack of interesting decoration often resulted in a boring, monotonous cityscape.

Most of these skyscrapers were rectangular slabs rising straight up from the ground floor to the top. In 1961, New York City amended the 1916 zoning law that required tall buildings to have setbacks, and other cities soon followed suit. Now that flourescent lighting and air conditioning were in use everywhere, setbacks were no longer needed to provide office workers with sufficient light and air.

Instead of setbacks, the new zoning regulations encouraged owners and architects to surround their office towers with broad, open plazas like the one in front of the Seagram Building. In return, the regulations permitted builders to add a few more floors to the height of their skyscrapers.

Open plazas looked attractive in architectural drawings. But too often in reality they proved to be merely vast stretches of empty pavement with nothing to look at, and no place to sit down.

In older skyscrapers that bordered on the sidewalk, the ground floors generally contained shops and restaurants. The plazas of the new skyscrapers usually led only to the lobby, or perhaps to a bank. Unless someone had business in the building, there was no reason

The Seagram Building (David Anderson)

to approach it. As a result a certain deadness came over the center of many cities despite the glitter of their new office towers.

In the late 1960s, many people in America turned their attention to environmental problems, and the new steel-and-glass skyscrapers were widely criticized. Ecologists pointed out that a cluster of tall buildings in a city often overburdens public transportation and parking lot capacities.

Skyscrapers are also lavish consumers, and wasters, of electric power. In one recent year, the addition of 17 million square feet (1.6 million square meters) of skyscraper office space in New York City raised the peak daily demand for electricity by 120,000 kilowatts—enough to supply the entire city of Albany, New York, for a day.

Glass-walled skyscrapers can be especially wasteful. The heat loss (or gain) through a wall of half-inch (1.25-cm) plate glass is more than ten times that through a typical masonry wall filled with insulation board. To lessen the strain on heating and air-conditioning equipment, builders of skyscrapers have begun to use double-glazed panels of glass, and reflective glasses coated with silver or gold mirror films that reduce glare as well as heat gain. However, mirror-walled skyscrapers raise the temperature of the surrounding air and affect neighboring buildings.

Skyscrapers put a severe strain on a city's sanitation facilities, too. If fully occupied, the two World Trade Center towers in New York City would alone generate 2.25 million gallons (8.5 million liters) of raw sewage each year—as much as a city the size of Stamford, Connecticut, which has a population of more than 109,000.

Environmentalists stress the many dangers that people living and working in and around today's tall buildings are exposed to. Skyscrapers distort the winds, causing downdrafts at street level that may blow people off their feet. If a fire starts in a skyscraper that does not have an adequate sprinkler system, deadly smoke and flames can quickly sweep up through elevator shafts, air-conditioning ducts, and mail chutes, trapping the workers inside. Those who work and live in high-rise office and apartment buildings are more vulnerable to thieves and muggers, who can escape easily via the many elevators and flights of stairs.

Skyscrapers also interfere with television reception, block bird flyways, and obstruct air traffic. In Boston in the late 1960s, some people even feared that shadows from skyscrapers would kill the grass on Boston Common.

Still, people continued to build skyscrapers for all the reasons that they have always built them—personal ambition, civic pride, and the desire of owners to have the largest possible amount of rentable

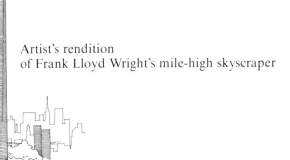

Artist's rendition
of Frank Lloyd Wright's mile-high skyscraper

space. And some architects envisioned structures much taller than any we know even today.

In 1956, the famous architect Frank Lloyd Wright designed a mile-high (1.6-km), spear-shaped skyscraper for Chicago's lakefront. The 528-story project might have been engineered, but it was eventually abandoned because of the huge problems involved in moving supplies, services, and an estimated 130,000 people in and out of the gigantic building each day.

Later, the Italian-American architect Paolo Soleri produced designs for future cities called "arcologies" that would be contained in a few towering air-conditioned buildings two or three miles (3.2-4.8 km) high. Around these great structures, to be located in the deserts of the Southwest, the land would be left in its natural, undeveloped state. Soleri claimed that arcologies would be the best way to combat the problems of overpopulation and urban decay, but he never actually built any.

Projects like these remained only visions in their creators' minds, and it wasn't until 1970 that the Empire State Building was finally replaced as the tallest building in the world by the World Trade Center in New York City.

8 : HIGHER AND HIGHER

Rising alongside the Hudson River, the 110-story towers of the World Trade Center look like two tall aluminum boxes standing on end. They dominate a 16-acre site that also includes a custom house, two shorter office buildings, a great central plaza with a fountain, and a hotel. Beneath the plaza is a grand concourse filled with shops, like the concourse under Rockefeller Center. To provide for ease of transportation, the concourse is linked with three subway lines and a railroad.

Unusual solutions were found to some of the problems involved in the construction of the World Trade Center. As excavation proceeded, concrete walls three feet (90 cm) thick and 70 feet (21 m) deep turned the building site into a giant empty bathtub with the waters of the nearby Hudson River kept on the outside.

In most skyscrapers, a skeleton of steel supports the structure and the walls merely contain the windows. But the World Trade Center

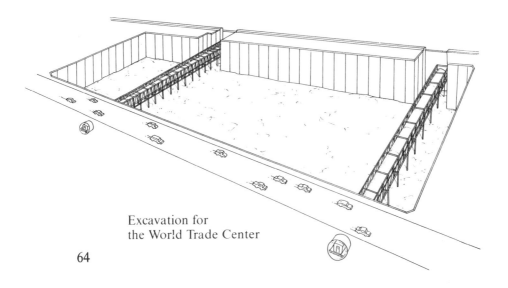

Excavation for
the World Trade Center

towers are different—their outer walls carry most of the buildings' weight loads, and provide the resistance to winds. The walls can do this because they consist of closely spaced vertical steel columns, tied together by massive horizontal spandrel beams that girdle the towers at every floor.

The World Trade Center also features a unique elevator system. Because the twin towers are so tall, the buildings have three lobbies—one on the concourse level, another on the 44th floor, and the topmost one on the 78th floor. Express elevators from the concourse, each with a capacity of 55 persons, and the fastest of their kind yet built, serve the two upper lobbies, or "skylobbies," as they are called. There the passengers transfer to local elevators to ascend to their desired floors higher up.

Not everyone who works in the World Trade Center likes the elevator system, however. One secretary, describing her daily routine of traveling on a crowded subway to the World Trade Center, and then on a crowded express elevator up to the 44th-floor skylobby, and finally on a crowded local elevator up to her 60th-floor office, said, "First I have a long horizontal commute on the subway—and then I have a long vertical commute on the elevators."

More than most skyscrapers, the World Trade Center has attracted people willing to risk their lives in order to prove their skill and daring.

Early in the morning of August 7, 1974, a young French high-wire artist, Philippe Petit, spent over 45 minutes on a 131-foot-long (40-m) steel cable strung between the twin towers of the World Trade Center, 110 stories above the ground. As spectators in the streets held their breath, Petit walked and ran back and forth across the wire while holding a 20-foot-long (6-m) balancing pole. He got down on one knee, bowed twice to those watching below, and at one point lay flat on the inch-wide (2.5-cm) cable and gazed up at the sky. He was finally persuaded to return to the roof of one of the towers by a policeman who shouted, "Get off of there or I'll come out and we'll both go down!"

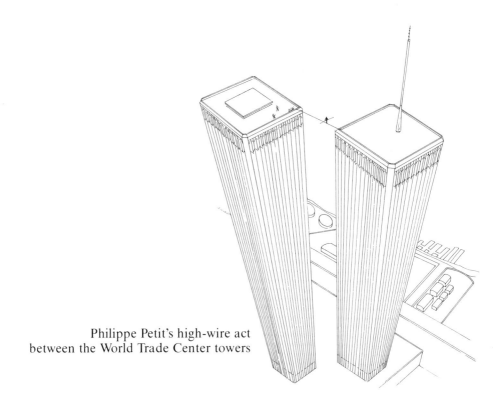

Philippe Petit's high-wire act between the World Trade Center towers

Later, at the police station, Petit explained how he and a friend had sneaked past guards at the World Trade Center with their equipment and spent the night before hidden on the roof. When asked why he had wanted to perform the stunt, Petit said, "If I see three oranges I have to juggle. And if I see two towers I have to walk." In 1971 he had walked on a wire strung between the towers of Notre-Dame Cathedral in Paris, and in 1973 he had repeated the performance between the towers of the Harbour Bridge in Sydney, Australia.

Almost three years after Philippe Petit's high-wire act, another young daredevil, George Willig, performed an equally dangerous stunt on the World Trade Center. At 6:30 A.M. on May 25, 1977, Willig, an amateur mountain climber, approached the south tower wearing climbing boots and a specially designed harness, and carrying grappling hooks. Before anyone could stop him, Willig began climbing the northeast corner of the building, where there were notches in the walls for window-cleaning equipment.

Willig paused at the 75th floor, leaned back against his harness, munched a doughnut, and gave his autograph to two police officers who had been lowered from the roof on an enclosed platform. He refused to join the officers on the platform, however, and kept on climbing. At 10:00 A.M., three and a half hours after he had started up the building, Willig finally reached the roof. There he was arrested and charged with disorderly conduct, reckless endangerment, criminal trespass, and climbing a building without a permit.

The World Trade Center reigned for only four years as the world's tallest building. In 1974, it was topped by the Sears Tower in Chicago,

The Sears Tower
(courtesy of Hedrich Blessing)

the city where the skyscraper had made its debut just 90 years before. Although both structures contain 110 stories, the Sears Tower is more than 100 feet (30.5 m) taller than the World Trade Center, rising 1,454 feet (443 m) above the streets of Chicago.

Clad in black aluminum, with bronze-tinted windows, the Sears Tower is actually nine buildings in one. It is composed of nine 75-by-75 foot (23-by-23-m) squares, each rising to a different height. This gives the building a more lively appearance than the unbroken boxes of the World Trade Center. The squares also help the tower to withstand the strong winds of Chicago without swaying. One hundred fourteen rock caissons support the 222,500-ton (200-million-kg) structure. Each is sunk over 150 feet deep, and is securely socketed into the bedrock beneath Chicago.

The Sears Tower has the most complete life-safety system ever devised for a high-rise building, with smoke detectors and automatic sprinklers to combat fires, and emergency generators in case of a power failure.

Near the top of the Sears Tower, 1,353 feet (412 m) above ground, is an enclosed observation deck called the "skydeck" which visitors can reach by express elevator in less than a minute. From the deck they can look out over Lake Michigan, stretching away to the east, and to the west they can see the beginning of the Great Plains.

Down below, and a little to the south, are the famous Chicago skyscrapers of the 1890s: the Monadnock Block, the Fisher Building, and, beyond them, the white tower of Louis Sullivan's Auditorium Building. From the skydeck of the Sears Tower none of these buildings seems very tall today. And, except for the Auditorium Building, none is included in the illustrated viewer's guide given to tower visitors.

Since 1974, no new skyscraper has challenged the Sears Tower in terms of height. But many striking and imaginative tall buildings have been erected since then in cities all across the United States.

In Boston, the John Hancock Tower, designed by I. M. Pei and Partners, rises 60 stories above Copley Square and reflects many of

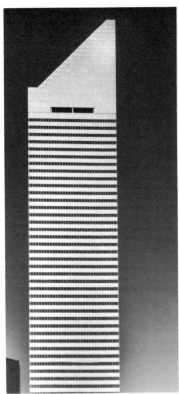 

Two views of the Citicorp Center (*left:* David Anderson; *right:* courtesy of Citicorp)

slanting roofs, seen together, look like a parrot's beak.

Another recent skyscraper with a slanting roof is the 59-story Citicorp Center, designed by Hugh Stubbins, which opened in New York City in 1977. When the technology has been perfected, the sloping crown of the building will house collectors for solar energy.

Four huge supporting columns, each 127 feet (39 m) tall, raise the tower of the Citicorp Center high above street level and provide space for a 9,000-square-foot (836-square-meter) sunken plaza with shade trees, a cascading waterfall, and, in the summer, garden tables and chairs.

To minimize the discomfort of normal building sway, a 400-ton (360,000-kg) concrete block in the Citicorp Center's crown is scientifically tuned to the building's movements. When the tower sways more than one foot (30 cm) a second, information is fed to a computer

The AT&T Building (Louis Checkman)

controlling the block, which is called a tuned mass damper, and it moves in the opposite direction to counteract and reduce the sway by 40 percent.

The IDS Center, the Pennzoil Building, and the Citicorp Center all contain shopping arcades on their ground floor levels. The arcades are enclosed so that they can be enjoyed by strollers and shoppers in all seasons of the year. They add to the attractiveness of the buildings, and are lively, colorful centers of human activity in the evenings and on weekends, as well as during the week. This is in sharp contrast to many of the skyscrapers of the 1950s and 1960s, whose barren plazas are usually deserted after 5:00 P.M.

In the late 1970s, Philip Johnson broke even more radically with the glass-box skyscrapers of the International Style that he had helped to introduce to the United States 50 years earlier. Going beyond his

The Pittsburgh Plate Glass Company (courtesy of Johnson/Burgee Architects)

designs for the IDS Center and the Pennzoil Building, Johnson drew plans for a new skyscraper for the American Telephone and Telegraph Company that would feature an 80-foot (24-m) entrance arch and, at the top, a 30-foot-high (9-m) triangular pediment with a large cutout circle in the middle. Critics immediately compared the design for the top of the building to the top of a grandfather clock or an antique highboy. They labeled it a "Chippendale skyscraper," after Thomas Chippendale, a famous English furniture designer of the 1700s.

After the AT&T Building, Johnson went on to design an even more controversial skyscraper for the home office of the Pittsburgh Plate Glass Company. Influenced by the Houses of Parliament in London, he applied the Gothic style to a 40-story skyscraper surrounded by five smaller buildings. Gothic arches provide the main entrance to the tower, and piers and columns rise to a crown of turrets and spires at the top.

With the Pittsburgh Plate Glass (PPG) headquarters, the skyscraper has come full circle, returning to the design approach used in the Woolworth Building and the Tribune Tower. The only difference is that the new skyscraper is clad in the mirror glass of today, rather than the terra cotta or stone of the past.

9 : SKYSCRAPERS IN THE FUTURE

What is likely to be the future of skyscrapers? Will new ones challenge the height records set by the Sears Tower and the World Trade Center? At the same time, will outstanding skyscrapers of the past be saved from the wrecker's ball?

Today, preservation groups all across the United States are working hard to make sure that the answer to the last question will be yes. Sometimes they have been too late, as in the case of New York's Singer Building, in 1908–09 the tallest building in the world—it was torn down in 1967. But they succeeded in St. Louis, where the National Trust for Historic Preservation, working in collaboration with the National Heritage Corporation, led a campaign to save Louis Sullivan's historic Wainwright Building.

When the two organizations learned that the Wainwright Building was about to be sold to a developer who planned to demolish it, they put a down payment on it themselves. This gave them time to search for a buyer who would agree not to tear down the building. Subsequently the State of Missouri purchased the building and restored it as part of a state office complex. Today the strong red-brick piers and beautifully decorated cornice of the Wainwright Building continue to capture the attention of pedestrians in downtown St. Louis.

As preservation campaigns to save downtown business districts have spread from city to city, more and more of these districts have come to be used as outdoor classrooms for the study of American history, art, architecture, and science. In Cambridge, Massachusetts, fourth- through eighth-grade students study the built urban environment—its textures, patterns, and shapes—and investigate the forces that have changed it over the years. In Birmingham, Alabama, students participating in the "Downtown Discovery Tour" are given guidebooks filled with photographs of terra cotta decorations and elaborate cornices. Then the students try to locate them on the four great turn-of-the-century skyscrapers grouped at the city's "Heaviest Corner."

Other cities are experimenting with similar programs, and in them downtown skyscrapers always play a major role. As school groups or adults on walking tours look up at the skyscrapers of the past, they get a better idea of their city's history. And as they gaze at the steel frames of new skyscrapers under construction, they can imagine what the city will look like in the future.

Will as many skyscrapers be built in the next 100 years as have been erected in the last 100? And will they climb even higher into the sky?

No one can answer either of those questions for certain. But as the population continues to increase, more office and apartment space will be needed. Technologically, it will be possible to build taller structures than those we know today—engineers are prepared to brace buildings with stiff exterior walls like those in the World Trade Center, and elevator manufacturers are confident that their vehicles can carry passengers up to at least 180 floors.

What will such future giants look like? That's difficult to predict. They may be designed in the tradition of the great skyscrapers of the past, in the so-called "Post-Modern Style" launched by Philip Johnson and other contemporary architects. Or their builders may return to the boxy, undecorated look of the skyscrapers erected by International Style architects like Mies van der Rohe. The one thing it's safe to predict is that the design of future skyscrapers will be heavily influenced, as the design of skyscrapers always has been, by changing times and changing tastes.

In terms of ecology, skyscrapers will probably always have critics like Lewis Mumford, who once wrote, "Actually, the skyscraper, from first to last, has been largely an obstacle to intelligent city planning and architectural progress. Its chief use has been to overcrowd the land for private financial advantage, at no matter what cost to the municipality, and to provide a costly means of publicity and advertisement."

Future skyscrapers will probably also have supporters like Philip Johnson, who has said, "To me, the drive for monumentality is as inbred in people as the desire for food. All cultures that can be called cultures have built monuments—that is, buildings of unusual size and expenditure of effort, that have aroused pride and enjoyment as well as utility."

Throughout history, people have erected tall structures—from the towers of medieval castles, to the lofty spires of Gothic churches, to the commercial skyscrapers of the last century. In the future, despite all the problems they create and the criticism they inspire, skyscrapers most probably will continue to be raised higher and higher into the sky.

Manhattan skyline at dusk
(David Anderson)

FABULOUS FACTS ABOUT FAMOUS SKYSCRAPERS

THE MONADNOCK BLOCK IN CHICAGO (1891)

At sixteen stories, the Monadnock Block was the tallest office building ever constructed entirely of masonry.

To support its height and weight, the masonry walls of the Monadnock Block were six feet thick at the base.

THE FISHER BUILDING IN CHICAGO (1896)

The steel framework for the Fisher Building's seventeen stories was erected in only a month, a record for the time. The entire building was ready for occupancy just nine months after ground was broken for the foundation.

When it was built, the Fisher Building was one of the tallest office buildings in the world, and the only one erected almost entirely without bricks. Terra cotta panels and glass covered its steel frame.

Two-thirds of the Fisher Building's surface was filled in with glass windows. This made people call it "a building without walls."

THE METROPOLITAN LIFE TOWER IN NEW YORK (1909)

Its design was patterned after the famous bell tower in St. Mark's Square in Venice, Italy. But the 50-story Metropolitan Life Tower is more than twice as high as the tower in Venice.

On the 26th floor of the tower is the largest four-faced clock in the world.

In 1909, radio pioneer Lee De Forest sent out the first long-distance radio message in the United States from the top of the tower. The signal reached as far as Milwaukee, Wisconsin, and Key West, Florida.

At the top of the Metropolitan Life Tower is a powerful beacon known as "the light that never fails." It has shone continuously since the building opened, except for three years during World War II when it was turned off to comply with dimout regulations.

THE WOOLWORTH BUILDING IN NEW YORK (1913)

The Woolworth Building has 60 stories. It might have had 79 or 80 stories with average-height ceilings, but the builder, Frank W. Woolworth, demanded high ceilings to go with the building's Gothic style. Some of the ceilings are 20 feet (6 m) high; none is lower than 11 feet (3.5 m).

There are over 30 acres (121,400 square meters) of floor space in the Woolworth Building, and over 5,000 windows.

The building's construction required 17 million bricks, 7,500 tons (6.8 million kg) of terra cotta, 53,000 pounds (24,000 kg) of bronze and iron hardware, and 87 miles (140 km) of electric wiring.

The Woolworth Building was the first skyscraper to have its own power plant. Four engines generate enough electricity to supply a city of 50,000 people on an average day.

THE TERMINAL TOWER IN CLEVELAND (1930)

The tower's foundation on bedrock is 130 feet (40 m) below the level of nearby Lake Erie.

There are 17,800 tons (16 million kg) of steel in the tower, 7.5 miles (12 km) of electrical wire, and 2,200 windows.

Three million cubic yards (2.3 million cubic meters) of earth were excavated for the entire Union Terminal group of buildings.

THE EMPIRE STATE BUILDING IN NEW YORK (1931)

Seventy-three elevators operate at speeds ranging from 600 feet to 1,200 feet (183–366 m) a minute in seven miles (11 km) of shafts.

There are 60 miles (96.5 km) of water pipe in the building, over 3,500 miles (5,633 km) of telephone and telegraph wire, and 6,500 windows that have to be washed twice a month.

Giant air-conditioners change the air throughout the building six times an hour.

From the observation decks, snow and rain can sometimes be seen falling up instead of down because of wind patterns around the building.

THE WORLD TRADE CENTER IN NEW YORK (1970–71)

Over a million cubic yards (765,000 cubic meters) of earth and rock were excavated to make way for the World Trade Center. The excavated material was placed in the Hudson River and created 23.5 acres (95,100 square meters) of new land.

The concrete used in the World Trade Center would have been enough to lay a sidewalk five feet (1.5 m) wide all the way from New York City to Washington, D.C.

The electrical wiring required for the twin towers would have reached from New York City to Mexico.

The plaza of the World Trade Center occupies five acres (20,200 square meters), more than the area of four football fields.

THE IDS CENTER IN MINNEAPOLIS (1972)

Excavation totaled 320,000 cubic yards (245,000 cubic meters), the equivalent of 1,020 average home basements.

Structural steel used in the IDS Center amounted to nearly 15,000 tons (13.6 million kg), enough for a Navy cruiser.

There are 42,614 panes of reflective glass in the IDS Center. This would be enough to provide two pairs of sunglasses for each resident of Minnesota, and one pair for each resident of North Dakota and South Dakota.

THE SEARS TOWER IN CHICAGO (1974)

Construction took four years, and during peak times 1,600 people worked on the project each day.

The tower contains enough concrete to build an eight-lane highway five miles (eight km) long.

If laid out on the ground, the black aluminum skin of the tower would cover 28 acres (113,000 square meters).

Six automatic window-washing machines clean the entire exterior of the Sears Tower eight times a year.

WHAT SOME ARCHITECTURAL TERMS MEAN

Art Deco style: The design style launched at the International Exposition of Decorative Arts in Paris in 1925. Skyscrapers in the Art Deco style often rise in steps, like Mayan temples, and are topped with one or more towers. They are ornamented with bands of brick, terra cotta, or metal in stylized floral patterns or geometric designs.

Beaux Arts style: A style of architecture developed in the late 19th and early 20th centuries by architects who studied at the École des Beaux Arts (School of Fine Arts) in Paris. Beaux Arts skyscrapers include such elements from the classical architecture of past centuries as columns, domes, and flying buttresses. Their surfaces are usually covered with elaborate stone or terra cotta decorations.

Column: A pillar that helps to support a building.

Cornice: A decorative molding at the top of a building wall. It can rise up above the wall or jut out from it—sometimes it does both.

Flying buttress: A supporting arch of masonry that curves out from the wall or roof of a building.

Foundation: The lowest part of a building. It usually rests in or on the earth or rock that supports the structure.

Gargoyle: A sculptural projection from the roof or wall of a building. Gargoyles are often in the form of distorted human faces or the heads of mythical beasts. They first appeared on Gothic churches in the Middle Ages and were used as drain spouts. Rainwater ran out of the carved mouths of the creatures, away from the building's walls.

Gothic style: Dominant in Europe in the 13th, 14th, and 15th centuries, the Gothic style reached its zenith in designs for great cathedrals. Their arched entrances, high arched roofs, and tall spires seemed to reach to the heavens.

International Style: The sleek streamlined style of architecture pioneered in the 1930s by Mies van der Rohe, Le Corbusier, and other architects. Skyscrapers in the International Style had little decoration, and their walls were usually covered with glass. Critics called such skyscrapers "glass boxes."

Load: There are two kinds of load on a building. *Dead load* is the total downward pressure of all the permanent elements—the walls, floors, elevators, etc.—in the structure. *Live load* is the downward pressure that may be added to the structure temporarily. The people who work in a skyscraper, or who visit it, are part of the building's live load.

Pediment: The triangular face of a roof, especially on buildings designed in the classical style of the ancient Greeks and Romans.

Pier: An upright structure that helps to support a building, either by itself or as part of a wall. A pier can be round or square, or other shapes, and can be made of stone, brick, concrete, or metal.

Skyscraper: A modern building of great height constructed on a steel skelton.

Spandrel: The panel of wall between structural columns, and between a windowsill and the top of the next window below it.

Terra cotta: Clay bricks that have been cast and fired. They are usually flatter and larger than regular bricks, and are covered with sculptured designs. On older skyscrapers, terra cotta panels were often used for decoration above entrances and in bands around the buildings. Sometimes terra cotta panels covered the entire surface of a skyscraper.

Right: the IDS Center (Richard W. Payne); *left:* the Pennzoil Building (courtesy of Johnson/Burgee Architects)

Boston's classic old buildings in the 10,344 glass panes of its curtain wall.

The Hancock Tower acquired an unwanted fame in 1972–73, when many of the original glass panes fell out due to temperature extremes and high winds. For a time, the temporary patches on its surface earned the building the nickname "Plywood Tower." Eventually the original walls were replaced with fully tempered safety glass half an inch (1.25 cm) thick. As a result of the bad experience with the Hancock Tower, models for new skyscrapers in other cities are now subjected to more stringent wind-tunnel testing than ever before.

Skyscrapers of the 1970s began to lose the glass-box look of skyscrapers built in the 1950s and 1960s. In 1972, the New York architectural team of Philip Johnson and John Burgee designed a 57-story skyscraper with eight sides of reflecting glass for the IDS (Investors Diversified Services) Center in downtown Minneapolis. The IDS Tower is now the tallest building between Chicago and San Francisco. Later, in 1976, the same team of architects designed the Pennzoil Building in Houston, twin 36-story glass towers in the shape of trapezoids with roofs that slant at a 45-degree angle. Some say that the two

BIBLIOGRAPHY

BOOKS FOR YOUNG READERS

Macaulay, David. *Unbuilding.* Boston: Houghton Mifflin Co., 1980.

———. *Underground.* Boston: Houghton Mifflin Co., 1976.

Younker, Richard. *On Site: The Construction of a High-Rise.* New York: Thomas Y. Crowell, 1980.

BOOKS FOR ADULTS

Blake, Peter. *Form Follows Fiasco.* Boston: Atlantic–Little, Brown, 1977.

———. *The Master Builders.* New York: W. W. Norton & Co., rev. ed. 1976.

Burchard, John, and Bush-Brown, Albert. *The Architecture of America: A Social and Cultural History.* Boston: Atlantic–Little, Brown, 1961.

Bush-Brown, Albert. *Louis Sullivan.* New York: George Braziller, 1960.

Cheney, Sheldon. *The New World of Architecture.* New York: Longmans, Green, 1930.

Chernov, V. *Moscow: A Short Guide.* Moscow: Progress Publishers, 1977.

Condit, Carl W. *The Chicago School of Architecture.* Chicago: University of Chicago Press, 1964.

Condon, George E. *Cleveland: The Best-Kept Secret.* Garden City, N.Y.: Doubleday & Co., 1967.

Eldredge, Joseph L. *Architecture Boston.* Barre, Mass.: Barre Publishing Co., 1976.

Fletcher, Sir Banister. *A History of Architecture on the Comparative Method.* New York: Charles Scribner's Sons, 1961.

Giedion, Sigfried. *Space, Time, and Architecture.* Cambridge, Mass.: Harvard University Press, 1963.

Goldberger, Paul. *The City Observed: New York.* New York: Vintage Books, 1979.

Hansen, Harry. *California: A Guide to the Golden State.* New York: Hastings House, 1967.

Huxtable, Ada Louise. *Kicked a Building Lately?* New York: Quadrangle, 1976.

James, Theodore, Jr. *The Empire State Building.* New York: Harper & Row, 1975.

Jordy, William H. *American Buildings and Their Architects.* New York: Anchor Books, 1972.

Koolhaas, Rem. *Delirious New York.* New York: Oxford University Press, 1978.

Krinsky, Carol Herselle. *Rockefeller Center.* New York: Oxford University Press, 1978.

Lorant, Stefan. *Pittsburgh: The Story of an American City.* Garden City, N.Y.: Doubleday & Co., 1964.

Mumford, Lewis. *Roots of Contemporary American Architecture.* New York: Reinhold, 1952.

Noble, Charles. *Philip Johnson.* New York: Simon & Schuster, 1972.

Robinson, Cervin, and Bletter, Rosemarie Haig. *Skyscraper Style.* New York: Oxford University Press, 1975.

Saylor, Henry H. *A Dictionary of Architecture.* New York: John Wiley & Sons, 1952.

Scully, Vincent, Jr. *Modern Architecture: The Architecture of Democracy.* New York: George Braziller, rev. ed. 1975.

White, Norval, and Willensky, Elliot. *AIA Guide to New York City.* New York: Macmillan Co., rev. ed. 1978.

Wrenn, Tony P., and Mulloy, Elizabeth D. *America's Forgotten Architecture.* New York: Pantheon Books, 1976.

INDEX

Aachen, medieval buildings of, 55
American Architect, 1
American Institute of Architects, 45, 53
"arcologies," 63
Art Deco style, 32–33, 38
   decoration in, 32–33, 34, 51
   piers in, 32–33
Associated Press Building, 50
AT&T Building, 72
Auditorium Building, 11, 68

Barclay-Vesey Building, 33–34, 51
Bauhaus school, 56, 57
Bayard Building, 16
Beaux Arts style, 16–18
Behrens, Peter, 55
Birmingham, Ala., 73–74
Blake, Peter, 56
Buffington, L. S., 2
Burgee, John, 69
Burne-Jones, Sir Philip, 19–20
Burnham, Daniel H., 8, 9, 18
Butter Tower, 30

California, earthquakes and construction in, 28, 35
Cambridge, Mass., 73
Cathedral of Learning, 28–29
Celanese Building, 53
Century City, 53
Chicago, Ill., 6–13, 29–31, 57–58, 67–68
   1871 fire of, 6
   Loop of, 7
Chicago Board of Trade Building, 34–35
Chicago Tribune, 29, 57
Chrysler Building, 38–39
Citicorp Center, 70–71
   solar energy and, 70
   tuned mass damper of, 70–71
Cleveland, Ohio, 35–37

"cloud scrapers," 2
Corbett, Harvey Wiley, 38
Corbin, John, 20
Cornwall, Dean, 52
Crystal Palace Exhibition, 4
cubistic style, 32

dirigibles, moored at Empire State Building, 44–45

earthquakes, 28, 35
Eastern Airlines Building, 50, 52
École des Beaux Arts, 16
elevators
   air cushioning of, 26
   early, 4–5
   high-speed, 1, 25–26, 50, 65
   limits of, 74
Ellithorpe, F. T., 26
Embarcadero Center, 53
Empire State Building, 39–47, 63, 77–78
   airplane crash into, 46
   awards of, 45
   deaths in construction of, 42
   elevators of, 44, 46, 47
   excavation for, 41
   filmmaking and, 45
   floodlights of, 47
   funding of, 40
   materials used for, 41, 42
   miniature railroad used in construction of, 42
   mooring mast of, 44–45
   observation decks of, 44, 45, 46, 47
   opening ceremony of, 42–44
   photographing of, 42
   planning of, 39–41
   rapid construction of, 42
   steel frame of, 41–42
   tourism and, 45, 47
   weather resistance of, 46

environmental effects, 47, 61–62, 74
European skyscrapers, 54–56
Exxon Building, 53

fire safety, 61, 68
Fisher Building, 10, 68, 76
Flatiron Building, 17–20
   criticism of, 19–20
   three-part structure of, 18–19
flying buttresses, 30
foundations
   floating, 8
   piers in, 8, 25
Fuller Building, 17

Galleria complex, 53
Gilbert, Cass, 23
glass
   double-glazed, 61
   falling, 69
   International Style and, 10, 56, 57–59, 61
   mirrored, 61, 72
Gothic style, 23, 28, 29, 30, 31, 54, 72
Great Depression, 40, 45, 54

"Heaviest Corner" (Birmingham), 74
Higbee Company department store, 35
Hine, Lewis W., 42
Hitchcock, Henry-Russel, 56
Hitler, Adolf, 56
Home Insurance Company Building, 3, 5, 7, 8
Hood, Raymond M., 30, 31, 48
Hoover, Herbert, 44
Hotel Cleveland, 35
Howells, John Mead, 30, 31

IDS Center, 69, 71, 78
Illinois Institute of Technology, 56, 57
International Building, 50, 52
International Exposition of Decorative Arts (1925), 32

International Style, 55–59, 71, 74
   European roots of, 55–56
   glass used in, 10, 56, 57–59, 61
   monotony and, 59, 61

Jenney, William Le Baron, 2–3
John Hancock Building (Chicago), 36
John Hancock Tower (Boston), 68–69
   falling glass of, 69
Johnson, Philip, 56, 69, 71–72, 74, 75
   International Style and, 56–57
   Post-Modern Style and, 69, 71–72, 74

King Kong, 45

Lake Shore Drive apartment buildings, 57–58, 59
Lamb, William F., 41
Lawrie, Lee, 52
Le Corbusier, 57
Lever House, 59
Los Angeles City Hall, 35

McGraw-Hill Building, 53
Manship, Paul, 49
masonry construction, 9
   steel frame construction vs., 2, 3
Medical Arts Building, 35
medieval buildings, 30, 55, 75
Mellon, Andrew W., 28
Metropolitan Life Insurance Company Tower, 20–23, 76
   clock of, 20–21
   observation deck of, 22–23
Mies van der Rohe, Ludwig, 55–56, 57–58, 59, 74
   Bauhaus and, 56
   skyscraper sketches of, 55–56
   student years of, 55
   in United States, 56, 57–58, 59
"mile-high building," 63
Ministry of Education and Health Building, 57

modernistic style, 32
Monadnock Block, 9–10, 68, 76
Moscow, "multistory buildings" of, 54
Mumford, Lewis, 34, 74
Museum of Modern Art, 56

Nazis, Bauhaus and, 56
New York Architectural League, 45
New York City, 16–27, 31–34, 38–53, 64–67
   rock base of, 16
   skyscraper concentration in, 38, 61
   zoning laws of, 31–32, 59–60

organic architecture, 12
Otis, Elisha, 4

Pei, I. M., and Partners, 68
Pennzoil Building, 69–70, 71
Peterhans, Walter, 57
Petit, Philippe, 65–66
Philadelphia Saving Fund Society Building, 57
piers
   in Art Deco style, 32–33
   in foundations, 8, 25
Pittsburgh, University of, 28
Pittsburgh Plate Glass (PPG) headquarters, 72
plazas, 49–50, 60–61, 70
"Plywood Tower," 69
portal bracing, 9–10, 25
Post-Modern Style, 74
preservation campaigns, 73–74
Prudential Building, 13

Radio City Music Hall, 52–53
   lobby of, 53
RCA Building, 50–52
   decorations of, 50–51
   lobby murals of, 51–52
   observation deck of, 50
   Rainbow Room and Grill of, 50
Rivera, Diego, 51–52
Rockefeller, John D., 48
Rockefeller Center, 48–53
   Atlas statue of, 52
   awards of, 53
   Channel Gardens of, 48–49
   Christmas trees of, 49–50
   lobbies of, 51–52
   modern expansion of, 53
   Prometheus statue of, 49
   Radio City Music Hall of, 52–53
   RCA Building of, 50–52
   Rockefeller Plaza of, 50
   sunken plaza of, 49–50
   underground concourses of, 52
Rockefeller family, 48, 52
Rookery, 7–8
Roosevelt, Franklin D., 44
Root, John Wellborn, 8, 9, 18
Russ Building, 28

Saarinen, Eliel, 31, 34
Saint-Saëns, Camille, 20
sandhogs, 36
Seagram Building, 59, 60
   detailed planning of, 59
Sears Tower, 67–68, 78
   foundation of, 68
   observation deck of, 68
   safety systems of, 68
Sert, José Maria, 52
setback construction, 31–32, 35, 41, 50, 60
shopping arcades, 71
Singer Building, 20, 73
skyscrapers
   aircraft and, 44–45, 46
   ambitions and, 5, 16, 62
   city-within-a-city, 48
   definitions of, 1
   early, height of, 1–2
   environmental effects of, 47, 61–62, 74
   European, 54–56
   fire safety and, 61, 68
   future of, 74–75
   medieval buildings and, 30, 55, 75
   "multistory buildings" vs., 54

skyscrapers *(cont.)*
  preservation of, 73–74
  real estate prices and, 5
  setback construction of, 31–32, 35, 41, 50, 60
  steel frame construction of, 2–3
  utilities and, 61
solar energy, 70
Soleri, Paolo, 63
Stalin, Joseph, 54
Standard Oil Building, 28
steel frame construction, 2–3
  masonry construction vs., 2, 3
stock market crash, 40
Stubbins, Hugh, 70
stunts, 65–67
Sullivan, Louis Henri, 11–13, 16, 31, 73
  theories about skyscrapers of, 12–13, 23

terra cotta panels, 10, 13, 73
Time-Life Buildings, 50, 53
Tribune Tower, 29–31
  criticism of, 31
  design competition for, 29–30
  famous stones of, 30–31
  Gothic style of, 29, 30, 31
tuned mass dampers, 70–71

Union Bank Building, 35
Union Terminal Tower, 36–37, 77
  danger in construction of, 36–37
  dedication of, 37

United Nations Secretariat Building, 58–59
utilities, 61

Van Sweringen, Mantis and Oris, 36, 37
Voorhees, Gmelin and Walker, 33

Wainwright Building, 13
  preservation of, 73
Wells, H. G., 20
Willig, George, 66–67
Wilson, Woodrow, 26, 42
Woolworth, Frank W., 23, 26–27
  office of, 26
Woolworth Building, 23–27, 77
  dedication of, 26
  elevators of, 25–26
  foundation of, 24–25
  Gothic style of, 23
  interior of, 23–24, 26
  restoration of, 27
  weather resistance of, 25
World Trade Center, 1, 64–67, 68, 78
  elevators of, 1, 65
  excavation of, 64
  outer walls of, 65, 74
  stunts and, 65–67
Wright, Frank Lloyd, 63

zoning laws, 31–32, 59–60